GETTING INTO COLLEGE

with Julia Ross

FINDING THE RIGHT FIT
AND
MAKING IT HAPPEN

GETTING INTO COLLEGE

with Julia Ross

Finding The Right Fit
and
Making It Happen

Julia Ross
Professional Tutoring, LLC

LTM
BOOKS

LTM Books

352 Seventh Avenue

New York, NY 10001

LTM Books is an imprint of LifeTime Media, Inc.

Visit our website at www.lifetimemedia.com or www.ltmbooks.com

Neither LifeTime Media nor any of its goods or services are in any way affiliated with, associated with, sponsored by or approved by Lifetime Networks, Lifetime television, or Lifetime Entertainment Services

ISBN: 978-0-9823975-3-4

Library of Congress Control Number: 2009938654

All LTM Books and LifeTime Media titles are available for special promotions, premiums, and bulk purchase. For more information, please contact the manager of our sales department at 212-631-7524 or sales@lifetimemedia.com

Distributed to the trade by Perseus Book Group
To order books for the trade call 1-800-343-4499

Printed in the United States of America

10.9.8.7.6.5.4.3.2.1

To all the Professional Tutoring students past, present, and future.
May all of your dreams come true.

CONTENTS

FOREWORD

Here I sit, in tears, completely panicked. Not only am I facing my senior year of high school but I have the daunting task of looking for a college that is the right fit for me (not my parents). I have to fit in class work, essays for college admissions, and applications for college while enjoying my senior year. My parents are driving me crazy because all they talk about is college. Sometimes a little outside guidance is necessary, and this book is just that.

Finding the right fit can be difficult, but not impossible. Do not misunderstand, no college is perfect; however, the likelihood of searching for and finding the right college is possible. The teenage years are frustrating, caught between childhood and adulthood; the simplest tasks can seem impossible. Of course, asking parents for help is something I really do not want to do; at least, I'd never admit to wanting parental help. With everything that needs to be completed before even applying to colleges including tours, interviews, and resumes, stress can build up and become unbearable. The largest problem that occurs when searching for a college is maintaining your identity and reassuring yourself that all will work out.

Organizing what I need is one of the hurdles that I have to overcome in the next few months. Figuring out what type of college environment I want to be in is the next step in the process. Although you may have encountered friends or family members that will share their triumphant and horrific college search stories, remember, yours will be different. However, the only way to ensure the difference is this book. This book will be the guiding light needed by you and your parents to remain sane through this insane process of finding the "right" colleges and getting in. Nevermind paying for four years of advanced education.

Finding the right fit is needed to ensure success, but most importantly happiness. If you are unhappy, it is hard to be successful. Trust me, I know from experience; sophomore chemistry was a killer. College is the next step toward your future, not your parents' future, your future. I tend to emphasize the fact that this is your decision, because I know that all parents want the best for us, even though they may appear overbearing at times. I am also in the middle of this overwhelming process. Still I always feel relieved after reading even a chapter of this book. This book will allow you to escape the overwhelming feelings that may envelope you at times. This book will allow you to discover where you want to be and what you want to do in life. The majority of students looking at colleges have no idea what they want to major in or what they want in life. But, that is perfectly normal. Discover where you want to be with the help of this book, and the rest will come with time. Looking for the right school is important, but with the right outlook, it can also be fun. So, de-stress and enjoy the moments ahead, because this is only the beginning.

~ Samantha Mullen, at the beginning of senior year

Chapter 1

The College Selection Journey

. . . .

Does it seem like everyone else around you is all set with their life's plans? Does it seem as though you are the only person who has no idea of how to begin your college search process? Or do you sometimes feel that it might be best to forgo the college route and just join the Marines? Call yourself normal. Every student and parent with whom I have worked over the past fifteen years in College Coaching has had the same doubts and fears. I will share some of those stories in this book and I promise that all of the stories end well, with students happily settled in college. It is getting there that is hard, more emotionally-charged than anything else.

Getting into College with Julia Ross: Finding the Right Fit and Making it Happen will give you the tools to do just that , and the best part of this book is that it is designed to help all types of students. The process and strategies outlined will work for middle-of-the-road B students, mid-range C struggling students, and the all-A- superstars.

IN THIS CHAPTER

- Meet Colin, Grace and Ally, three ordinary students. Follow their extraordinary successes

- Timelines designed to guide you through your own successful college selection journey

Will all of these students get into Harvard or Yale? Absolutely not. Do they all want to go to Harvard or Yale? Again, absolutely not! We tend to get caught up in the brand name of colleges just as we do in the brand name of cars and clothing. The goal of *The College Coaching Handbook* is to help students identify colleges that meet their individual needs (academically, socially, athletically, and financially). Yes, you are in the driver's seat. You will choose colleges that will fit you! In Chapter 2, you will read about decision criteria, take a survey and develop your very own college list. Chapter 3 will help you understand the Numbers Game: test scores and GPA. It will help you to calibrate your "safety", "attainable", and "reach" schools, so that you can develop a realistic list of colleges to visit and submit applications.

Of course, the next question is how to make the colleges want you. Right? Once you have developed a list of colleges with appropriate admissions standards, you will give a lot of thought to what you have to offer these colleges. The admissions process, from the colleges' point of view, is no secret. Colleges are looking to develop a community of students; students who are leaders, musicians, athletes, researchers, etc. They want to fill their classes with a diversity of interests and talents.

In Chapter 4, you wil! work on packaging yourself to present to the colleges. Just as your parents develop a resume or fill out a job application listing their experience and skills, you will also. It is about packaging – not with glitter and bows and untruths. Instead, you will work with your parents, teachers, mentors and guidance counselors to develop a glowing student resume. Yes, you can glow too!

Your student resume will accompany your requests for recommendations. Your resume will help your teachers, guidance counselors, coaches or family friends to write about what a great addition you will be to the college community.

Chapter 5 will help you fill out those all-important college applications. Your student resume will help you to fill out your applications; it will remind you of your achievements to include on the application. This chapter will also help to unravel the complexities of Early Decision, Early Action, and Rolling Admissions Plans, among others. Chapter 6 will help you to choose potential recommenders and write letters requesting recommendations.

In Chapter 7, you will face the task of writing the dreaded college essay. In addition to providing an overview and list of do's and don'ts, the chapter includes essays ranging from two full pages (1000 words) to the short answer (200) word essay. You will surely enjoy these essays as they range from the comical to the tear-jerker. You may be surprised to find out that none of these great essays was written by an academic superstar and at least two were written by students in the low-C range.

You will learn about interviewing, visiting college campuses, and "romancing" the admissions officer in Chapter 8. College admissions officers are people, too; they respond to students who are excited about their schools. They want to fill their classes with young people who are passionate about attending. No college admissions counselor wants to know that a student considers their individual college a safety school, only a backup.

Chapter 9 will support the U.S. Service Academy and Reserve Officer Training Corps (ROTC) candidate. This chapter also includes samples of athletic and arts resumes.

Chapter 10 is the pièce de rèsistance. After your successful search, packaging and applications, you will look at scholarships and financial aid. As unbelievable as it may seem, colleges and universities are looking to give away money, even in this financial climate! Many, many private schools offer merit awards (not need-based financial aid) in their initial interviews or even in their pre-application letters. Many of my students find that they can attend a private college for the same or nearly the same cost as their in-state public school. In addition, private and public colleges across the nation offer merit awards to students who qualify for their honors programs.

Best of luck. Keep in touch with me through this process at ProfessionalTutoring@cox.net or online at www.JuliaRossProfessional Tutoring.com.

PARENTAL INVOLVEMENT

How do I motivate this surly lunk of a teenager? This is the question that plagues many parents. If you are dealing with a pouting, moody, and uncooperative teenager who responds to your gentle nudges with uncommunicative silences, you have raised a normal teenager! If, on the other hand, you are off to a smooth start, congratulations; you are in the top one percent of the nation.

I promise this process will become easier...quickly. The toughest part for everybody is getting started. Begin with leafing through the book and the first two chapters. As you focus on the steps in the college search process, you and your son or daughter will stop staring each other down and begin to tackle the task at hand.

Set a wide net in order to look at lots of schools. Plan on your student applying to eight or nine schools to offer a good balance of safety, attainable and reach schools. Although this process seems over-whelming at the outset, it does end up being positive and, surprisingly, enjoyable.

If I can offer a single caution, it would be not to believe everything that you hear. Urban legends and gossip abound through the college admissions process. It is true that some colleges, like the Ivy League and the top public universities, are very selective. These schools do deny many, many applicants, even many applicants with top credentials. For every school that denies 80-90 percent of applicants, there is another that accepts 80, 90, even 100 percent of applicants. There are almost 4000 colleges in the United States. There is a college, in fact many college possibilities, for EVERY STUDENT.

With the idea of caution in mind, be aware that students and parents inflate their numbers and, frankly, make up stories and lie. Your student's college search and application processes are private. Filter carefully what you hear and keep your eye on the ball: securing admission at four to five colleges/universities that meet your student's needs and goals. This is not a neighborhood competition.

Finally, step back and let your child shine. You will see your student through adult eyes, measured by deans and administrators who no longer consider the students children but rather young adults. Enjoy!

STUDENT INVOLVEMENT

Well, here you are, on your path to adulthood. And, no, you cannot turn around and you soon won't want to. You are standing at the edge of adulthood and shaping your future. College should be among the best four years of your life. You will be on your own for the first time in your life, most likely living away from home with built-in friends. Your professors will treat you like an adult; no longer will you need a hall pass to go to the bathroom or face detention if you miss an assignment.

The college application process does not have to be difficult. You can actually enjoy this journey. One key? Remember that it is your journey. Not your parents'. Not your friends'. Not your teachers' or neighbors' or anyone else's. Your goal will be to gain admission to colleges and universities that stoke your fire academically, socially, athletically and financially.

So take pride in yourself. Take the lead in this process. Do your own research. Write your own essay; ask for editing help after you are finished writing a good draft. Contact the admissions offices yourself and develop a relationship with the staff, that is separate from your parents.

OUR THREE STUDENTS: COLIN, GRACE AND ALLY

We follow three students through the book, none of whom would have had the success that s/he found without this process. Colin, our future doctor, had lackluster grades his first two years, so lackluster, in fact, that with a superstar junior year (GPA-over 3.7), his three year cumulative GPA barely crossed the 3.0 (B) line. Nevertheless, Colin had an epiphany after his sophomore year; he found in himself the calling to become a doctor. Colin threw himself into school work, volunteered in specific medical capacities and polished his resume. Now, Colin is just starting his second year at the University of Pittsburgh with a 60% merit scholarship! His bang-up essay was so impressive, that he received a letter of commendation.

Our second student, Grace, was told by an educational psychologist (Ph.D.) that as an elementary student college would most likely be out of her reach and to plan for a vocational education. Fortunately, Grace never paid attention to this "advice." Like Colin, Grace bloomed late. She took on leadership roles both in and out of school, began her own business, got serious about studying some time in her junior year and packed her senior year with IB (honors) classes. By October of her senior year, the colleges were chasing her down with scholarship offers. By December the scholarship offers had reached over $200,000 over four years! Was Grace's case a miracle? Not at all; Grace followed the process in this book. Like Colin, she developed a strong student resume and "romanced the admissions officers" by showing her interest and keeping in touch. In October of her senior year, Grace accepted a major leadership program and scholarship, one of 250 students out of an applicant pool of 9,000.

Our third student, Ally, is a great young woman, with average grades, weak SAT scores, Division III Lacrosse skills and a big personality. Ally has always found focusing in school a bit difficult and has to work hard to edge near a 3.0 average. Nevertheless, Ally came out of the box running at the end of her junior year. She developed a strong resume which highlighted her athletic and extracurricular skills. Ally talked to coaches, attended showcases and visited colleges. By the spring of her senior year, she had several college admissions and several scholarship offers. Again, Ally found the scholarship possibilities by making sure to visit colleges in which she was interested. Whenever possible, she interviewed to gain a footing with her very likeable personality. In the end, Ally turned down in-state tuition at a private school, accepting instead one of her state public universities.

While Grace and Colin had good resumes, reasonable grades and fairly strong SAT scores, neither would have stood out tremendously in a pile of college applications. Ally, on the other hand, had the deck somewhat set against her with weaker grades and SAT scores. What set these three students apart was their consistent contact with the admissions offices of their choice schools. They interviewed; they toured campuses; they attended open houses; they forwarded student resumes and kept in touch. In essence, they cultivated relationships and moved from a set of numbers to living, breathing, eager future college students. You can do this too!

OPTIMAL JUNIOR/SENIOR TIMELINE

May: **Read Chapter 1 of** *Getting Into College With Julia Ross*

_____ 1. Take the SAT Reasoning and/or the ACT Exam (College Board.org or ACT.org) as soon as possible.

_____ 2. Register, if necessary, for the SAT Subject Exams.

_____ 3. Request and pick up Unofficial School Transcripts with 3-year cumulative GPA from the guidance office (available for pick up usually within a week of the last day of school).

June 1 to 15: Read Chapters 2 and 3

_____ 1. Take the SAT Reasoning Exam or the ACT.

_____ 2. Make copies of your transcript, SAT/ACT scores.

_____ 3. Set up a time for parents and student to spend one hour together completing the Professional Tutoring College Selection Survey.

_____ 4. Develop preliminary college list: handwritten is fine; using college guide books, CollegeBoard.com's college search feature, teachers, counselors, etc.

_____ 5. Develop a college selection spreadsheet – using Excel or another similar spreadsheet – Follow the formats at the end of Chapter 2. This will take four to five hours. Save the spreadsheet for later updates.

June 16 to June 30: Read Chapters 5 and 8

_____ 1. Review College Selection Spreadsheet with parents.

_____ 2. Refine College Selection Spreadsheet with more data and/or additional schools.

_____ 3. Purchase: small portable filing box, different colored file folders and labels, large envelopes (10 x 12).

_____ 4. Visit the websites of your target schools:

- Verify the information in the College Selection Spreadsheet
- Download an application from each college
- File applications in separate, labeled folders
- On the outside of each folder, list requirements for each application
- Plan college visits
- Set up interviews and auditions and contact coaches and/or professors, if appropriate
- Register on NCAA.com, if appropriate
- Continue your college research and visits all summer and fall

July 1 to July 15: Read Chapters 4 and 6

_____ 1. Write Student Resume and Athletic/Arts Resumes (Chapter 9) as applicable. Use computer spelling and grammar checks.

_____ 2. Have an adult review the resume(s).

_____ 3. Choose "Recommenders".

_____ 4. Write Recommendation Request Letters.

_____ 5. Have someone review your Recommendation Request Letters. Make changes, as appropriate.

_____ 6. Send Recommendation Requests via U.S. mail, email or preferably, deliver them yourself.

July 16 to July 31: Read Chapter 7

_____ 1. Outline and write a first draft of all required essays and short answer questions.

_____ 2. Give yourself a couple of days away from your essay, then proofread, edit and polish your essay.

_____ 3. Ask several people (parents, counselor, and teacher) to review your essay and to provide comments.

_____ 4. Finalize your essay. Make sure you stayed within each school's length guidelines ($\pm10\%$).

_____ 5. Finalize list of target colleges (preferably eight schools – three safety, three attainable and two reach).

August 1 to August 31: Read Chapter 5
(for the second time)

_____ 1. Fill out all applications by hand. Highlight questions that need further research.

_____ 2. Complete application by hand. Have another person carefully proofread the draft of your college application.

_____ 3. Finish all essays and short answer questions. Proofread again !!

_____ 4 Complete each college application online. Before sending, PROOFREAD IT VERY CAREFULLY, comparing it to your hard copy filled out by hand.

_____ 5. If possible, work with your high school to have your official transcripts sent to the colleges to which you are applying. If the school office is closed, make this request the first week of September.

_____ 6. Register for October SAT/ACT Subject exams, if appropriate. Remember that it is best to take no more than two at a time. If necessary, register for one to two additional SAT Subject exams in November.

September: Read Chapters 9 and 10

_____ 1. Request secondary school reports from the guidance or career office in your school. These are different from your high school transcripts. Use the correct forms and expect three weeks of lead time.

_____ 2. Research merit aid, honors and other programs at your target schools.

_____ 3. Register for a FAFSA pin at (FAFSA.ed.gov). Download last year's application as a baseline for your research.

_____ 4. January 1, the FAFSA forms are available online for most states. Complete as necessary. Be aware that some colleges require this form to be completed even for merit aid.

_____ 5. If applicable, begin filling out these forms by hand. Take note of all of the requirements and begin the recommendation request process, write essays, set up interviews, plan to attend scholarship contest weekends at each school.

October:

_____ 1. Follow up with your school's guidance or career office to make sure that all of your secondary school reports were sent.

_____ 2. Follow up with each of the colleges to which you applied to make sure that they have received all of the required application materials for your packet.

_____ 3. Keep in contact with admissions counselors to indicate your continued interest.

CATCHING UP SENIOR TIMELINE

September: Read Chapter 1 of *Getting Into College*
                      with Julia Ross

_____ 1. Register to take the SAT Reasoning and/or the ACT Exam (CollegeBoard.org or ACT.org) as soon as possible.

_____ 2. Register, if necessary, for the SAT Subject Exams.

_____ 3. Request and pick up Unofficial School Transcripts with 3-year cumulative GPA from the guidance office.

October 1 to 15: Read Chapters 2 and 3

_____ 1. Take the SAT Reasoning Exam or the ACT.

_____ 2. Make copies of your transcript, SAT/ACT scores.

_____ 3. Set up a time for parents and student to spend one hour together completing the Professional Tutoring College Selection Survey.

_____ 4. Develop preliminary college list – handwritten is fine - using college guide books, CollegeBoard.com's college search feature, teachers, counselors, etc.

_____ 5. Develop a college selection spreadsheet – using Excel or another similar spreadsheet – Follow the formats at the end of Chapter II. This will take four to five hours. Save the spreadsheet for later updates.

October 16 to 31: Read Chapters 5 and 8

_____ 1. Review College Selection Spreadsheet with parents.

_____ 2. Refine College Selection Spreadsheet with more data and/or additional schools.

_____ 3. Purchase: small portable filing box, different colored file folders and labels, large envelopes (10 x 12).

_____ 4. Visit the websites of your target schools:

   • Verify the information in the College Selection Spreadsheet

   • Download an application from each college

   • File applications in separate, labeled folders

   • On the outside of each folder, list requirements for each application

   • Plan college visits

   • Set up interviews and auditions and contact coaches and/or professors, if appropriate

   • Register on NCAA.com, if appropriate

   • Continue your college research and visits all fall and winter

November 1 to 15: Read Chapters 4 and 6

_____ 1. Write Student Resume and Athletic/Arts Resume (Chapter Nine), as applicable. Use computer spelling and grammar checks.

_____ 2. Have an adult review the resume(s).

_____ 3. Choose "Recommenders".

_____ 4. Write Recommendation Request Letters.

_____ 5. Have someone review your Recommendation Request Letters. Make changes, as appropriate.

_____ 6. Send Recommendation Requests via U.S. mail, email or preferably, deliver them yourself.

November 16 to 30: Read Chapter 7

_____ 1. Outline and write a first draft of all required essays and short answer questions.

_____ 2. Give yourself a couple of days away from your essay, then proofread, edit and polish your essay.

_____ 3. Ask several people (parents, counselor, and teacher) to review your essay and to provide comments.

_____ 4. Finalize your essay. Make sure you stayed within length guidelines ($\pm$10).

_____ 5. Finalize list of target colleges (preferably eight schools – three safety, three attainable and two reach).

December 1 to 15: Read Chapter 5 (for the second time)

_____ 1. Fill out all applications by hand. Highlight questions that need further research.

_____ 2. Complete application by hand. Have another person carefully proofread the draft of your college application.

_____ 3. Finish all essays and short answer questions. Proofread again!!

_____ 4. Complete each college application online. Before sending, PROOFREAD IT VERY CAREFULLY comparing it to your hard copy filled out by hand.

_____ 5. If possible, work with your high school to have your official transcripts sent to the colleges to which you are applying. Do this as early in December as possible as the colleges close for winter break earlier than most high schools.

_____ 6. Register for October SAT/ACT Exams, if appropriate. Remember that it is best to take no more than two at a time. If necessary, register for one to two additional SAT Subject exams in November.

_____ 7. Request secondary school reports from the guidance or career offices in your school. These are different from your high school transcripts. Use the correct forms and expect three weeks of lead time.

December 16 to 31:   Read Chapters 9 and 10

_____ 1. Research merit aid, honors and other programs at your target schools.

_____ 2. Register for a FAFSA pin at (FAFSA.ed.gov). Download last year's application as a baseline for your research.

_____ 3. January 1, the FAFSA forms are available online for most states. Complete as necessary. Be aware that some colleges require this form to be completed even for merit aid.

_____ 4. If applicable, begin filling out these forms by hand. Take note of all of the requirements and begin recommendation request process, write essays, set up interviews, and plan to attend scholarship contest weekends at each school.

January

_____ 1. Follow up with your school's guidance or career office to make sure that all of your secondary school reports were sent.

_____ 2. Follow up with each of the colleges to which you applied to make sure that they have received all of the required application materials for your packet.

_____ 3. Keep in contact with admissions counselors to indicate your continued interest.

Chapter 2

Developing Your Personal College List

· ·

DECISION CRITERIA

In developing your personal list of colleges for consideration, the objective will be to find the schools that will best fit your personality: academic, social, athletic and extracurricular. You will have many, many aspects of collegiate life to consider. While most parents and students focus on the academic match, Professional Tutoring's College Coaching Program looks into many other quantitative and qualitative issues. Major issues for consideration are listed below:

ADMISSIONS PROBABILITY

It is important to realistically evaluate your chances of acceptance at each school. In my experience, both students and parents over-rate the student's probability of acceptance.

Safety

The students' exam scores and grade point average (GPA) will both be above the average statistics listed and significantly higher than the minimums listed. In order for a college to qualify as a safety school, its average or median SAT scores (Critical Reading and Math scores only) for accepted students should be at least 100-150 points below the prospective student's scores. The ACT will be three to four points below your score. In addition, the average or median GPA should be at least two to three tenths of a point below the prospective student's GPA. Remember that you will have the greatest probability of securing merit scholarships from safety schools.

Attainable

The students' exam scores and GPA will be on par with the average statistics listed and higher than the minimums listed. What does on par mean? This means that the average or median SAT scores (Critical Reading and Math scores only) for accepted students at the target college or university will be within 50 to 70 points of the prospective student's SAT scores and within one to two points of the school's median ACT. The average GPA will be within one to two tenths of a point of the prospective student's. In the best case scenario, if the prospective student's SAT scores are slightly below the target university's averages, the student's GPA will be slightly above, thereby balancing the slightly lower SAT score or vice versa.

Reach

Either the students' exam scores and/or GPA are below the average statistics listed but as high as or higher than the minimums listed. A reasonable reach school will have SAT scores within approximately 100-150 points (Critical Reading and Math scores only) of the average accepted student. The ACT scores will be a maximum of four points beneath the prospective school's median ACT scores for admitted students and the school's reported average GPA will fall within .2 to .3 points of the interested student's GPA. If the university's exam scores and the GPA are both above these markers, and the student has no other major "hook" (athletics/disability/major recommendation), the college is most likely out of reach.

Balance

Professional Tutoring recommends that students have the following balance of schools:

- Three Safety Schools
- Three Attainable Schools
- Two Reach Schools

This balance will give the student the greatest probability of having four to six acceptances from which to select.

DISTANCE

Many students initially announce that they want to go as far from home as possible. Usually by the time that the college choices come in; many students realize that they do not want to be so far from home. Some questions to consider are:

1. How often do you want to come home?

2. How will you feel when you catch the flu and there is no way to get home (to Mom)?

3. Will you want to come home frequently or only two or three times per year (Thanksgiving, Winter and Spring Breaks)?

4. Are there relatives, family friends in certain areas close to colleges you would consider?

GEOGRAPHY

Geography will play a critical role in your college experience in more ways than distance from home. Transitioning to the first year away from home is not easy for most kids. For this reason, Professional Tutoring recommends that students choose a school that is a reasonable distance from home and is at least somewhat similar to their native area's culture. For example, a student who has grown up in the heart of New York City might find a small southern college in a rural area completely stifling. Generally, the farther south that one travels, the more conservative the culture is. In the northeastern seaboard, many city and suburban schools have a much more liberal value system. Another important factor is weather. Some students dream of going far north, imagining weekly, or even daily, snowboarding expeditions only to find out that the miserable winter lasts from October through April or May. There is a big difference between Arizona's idea of cold and the weather in Maine. It is crucial that a student be comfortable with distance, culture and weather, in order to be able to settle into the new environment and the higher academic expectations.

ENVIRONMENT

As with geography, the environment of the colleges will play an important role in students' experiences. Urban colleges have much to offer including convenient public transportation, access to an airport, train station, the arts and activities. Suburban schools will fit into the fabric of the local community with perhaps a main street and local activities and interests. Professors may be more available for outside of class activities. Rural colleges tend to have their own more-isolated identity. Very large schools may have less involvement with the local community, yet a very strong sense of school identity and spirit.

ACADEMICS

Do you want to go to the most selective school that will accept you or do you want to have a more balanced experience in college? Most students automatically respond, "the most selective." It is important to take into consideration how hard you want to work and what other activities interest you.

MAJORS

While some students have an idea of their eventual career path, many do not. If you have a "calling" and are sure of your eventual career, then you will want to carefully consider the college/university programs for your interest. One way to do this is to count the number of majors offered within your discipline. For example, a potential engineer may count the number of engineering majors offered at each potential school, comparing the depth of the major. Another measurement is the graduate programs offered. Does the university offer both masters and doctoral programs in your major? Finally, more and more universities are offering five-year combined bachelors/masters programs in fields such as nursing, education, architecture and engineering. Some schools are beginning to offer a bachelors/doctoral physical therapy degree. If you are sure of your career, these programs may best suit your needs. If you have not yet determined your major, you will want to evaluate the college/university's different course offerings for breadth. Do you think that you might want to major in some type of business/liberal arts/healthcare/science? You will want to have plenty of opportunities to try different courses to see what piques your interest over the first year or two that you are in college. Remember, most colleges do not require students to declare a major until the junior year.

STUDENT/FACULTY RATIO

Most college books and websites list each individual college's student/faculty ratio. A major complaint of undergraduates at large universities is the number of graduate students, many with poor English skills or very heavy accents, who teach undergraduate courses. The student/faculty ratio will give you a better idea of how many tenured/Ph.D. faculty teach students directly. This is also a question to pose in an admissions information session or an interview.

SPECIAL ED

If you have relied on a 504 Plan or an Individualized Education Plan, give careful consideration as to whether you will need support and accommodations in college. Some schools have stronger special education services to support students. Make sure to talk with your high school teachers and case manager in making this decision.

SIZE

In general, large universities offer more course, social and athletic choices. At the same time, many of the freshman and sophomore survey courses and labs are taught by graduate students and/or in large lecture halls with little individual attention. On the other side of the coin, small colleges and universities tend to offer students more individual attention but fewer overall course, social and athletic opportunities.

SINGLE SEX VS. CO-ED

The idea of a single sex school seems outrageous to many students. Nevertheless, nothing should be ruled out without some thought. The single sex schools (Hampden-Sydney, Sweetbriar, Smith, or Wellesley) have a lot to offer. Single sex schools tend to be older and well-financed with endowments, and are able to offer significant merit scholarships. Many offer merit scholarships beginning at a 3.0 GPA and a 1000 (Critical Reading and Math) SAT score. In addition, many single sex schools have a sister/brother school as well as lots of other colleges and universities close by.

MALE/FEMALE RATIO

As the national male/female ratio at American colleges has shifted to only 40% male, the face of the American university has changed. Take a look at the male/female ratio at each college you consider. I strongly recommend looking for a ratio as close to 50/50 as possible. The even balance of males and females makes college life more fun.

PUBLIC VS. PRIVATE

Since we have so many good public universities in the United States, many families loathe to consider private colleges and universities, often because of concern over the cost. The sticker price for private colleges can shock even the most sanguine parent! Before ruling out private colleges/universities, think about visiting a private college or two. Many will offer merit scholarships to students up-front, decreasing total costs often by 50% or more! As private schools tend to be smaller than public universities, they offer the attendant benefits.

PERSONALITY FIT

Similar to geographical considerations, a good personality fit between a student and a college/university is important. This qualitative consideration must be made by the student, not the parents, friends or anyone else. Only the potential student will be able to determine if s/he fits into the school's social and academic fabric. One of the best ways to test the fit is to spend a night or two at the prospective schools in a dorm with a student, especially with a student that is not a friend or acquaintance from home. Many admissions offices will help prospective students by setting up an overnight visit. Students will judge the fit almost entirely intuitively with considerations of the following:

1. Is the campus quiet and peaceful?

2. Is the campus active and exciting?

3. Do students seem happy and lively?

4. Is there too much or too little partying?

5. Do students study enough/too much/too little?

6. Are the bulletin boards full of activities?

CAMPUS LIFE

One measurable consideration is the number of students who commute to school from home and how many go home on the weekends. Another major issue to consider is the partying on-campus. Some schools have well-earned reputations. Many students are also attracted to older schools for their well-defined traditions.

GREEK LIFE

If you are not already familiar with the term "Greeks," it refers to fraternities and sororities. Many students dream about the "Greek Life" and parents recoil in horror as visions of the 80's movie, *Animal House,* surge through their imaginations. If you are interested in joining a fraternity or sorority, you should add this to your list of important quantifiable measurements, along with majors, costs, etc. Like any other campus activity, the Greek Life can be quantified. Check out the percentage of students who belong to fraternities and sororities.

HOUSING

Most four-year colleges and universities will offer housing for first-year students (freshmen) at a minimum. On-campus housing is provided in dormitories (generally double or triple rooms), apartments or townhouses. Make sure to tour the different dorms available when you visit colleges. In addition, check with the admissions office on housing policies; some schools require freshmen and/ or upperclassmen to live on-campus. Others do not even guarantee housing for freshmen.

ATHLETICS

Finally, sports play an important role on college campuses across the country, for both athletes and non-athletes. Obviously, athletes who wish to play in the NCAA arena will have to register with the NCAA Clearing House in the summer between their junior and senior years. Many other students want to be part of the school spirit and spectator sport opportunities that sports bring to colleges and universities across the country. The NCAA divides sports into three divisions, I, II and III, descending in order from most competitive to least. Generally, the well-known football and basketball schools play in the NCAA Division I conference. Beside the NCAA conference, there are several smaller conferences, including NAIA, as well as club teams which allow students to participate in athletics with less intensity.

FINANCES

First on every parent's mind is how to finance a four or more year college education. Please do not make cost one of your major criteria at this beginning stage. Many schools will meet or beat in-state tuition through financial aid; both merit aid, which generally does not consider family finances and need-based aid, which does require detailed family financial information.

COLLEGE SELECTION SURVEY:

Now it is your turn to apply your new-found college knowledge to yourself. You will use the 18 decision criteria that you just learned about to fill out the Professional Tutoring College Selection Survey, found in the next few pages. The survey follows the same path as the decision criteria beginning with the all-important statistical qualifications (test scores and grades). Use the chart on page 30 to evaluate your individual "Numbers Game" and determine the level of safety, attainable and reach schools appropriate for you. Next, you will look at five major categories:

1. Location: Distance, Geography and Environment

2. Academics: Academics, Majors, Student/Faculty Ratio, Special Education and Class Size

3. Social Life: Size of the Student Body, Single Sex vs. Co-ed, Male/Female Ratio, Public vs. Private, Personality Fit, Campus Life, Greek Life and Housing

4. Activities: Athletics and Activities

5. Finances

Make sure to refer back to our 18 Decision Criteria as you think about your needs and desires. The survey wraps up with the opportunity for you to fantasize about the college or colleges that would suit you perfectly.

Plan to spend an hour working through the survey with your parents and/or guidance counselor. I have designed the survey to help you to decide what is important to you. Think carefully. Your results will support you in narrowing your search and creating your own college selection spreadsheet. You are officially on your way to becoming a college student!

COLLEGE SELECTION SURVEY YOUR NUMBERS

GPA: _____

SAT Score: Date: _____

CRdg: _____ Math: _____ Total: _____

Writ: _____ Essay: _____ Total: _____

SAT Score: Date: _____

CRdg: _____ Math: _____ Total: _____

Writ: _____ Essay: _____ Total: _____

Best SAT Score: Date: _____

CRdg: _____ Math: _____ Total: _____

Writ: _____ Essay: _____ Total: _____

ACT Score Composite: Date: _____

Score: _____

ACT Score Composite: Date: _____

Score: _____

Best ACT Score: Date: _____

Score: _____

Admissions Probability

This will probably be your least favorite part of the survey, determining which schools to consider based on your grades and SAT scores. This page will help you to calculate SAT/ACT scores and grade point averages of your prospective Safety, Attainable and Reach Schools, as follows:

Admissions Probability Organizer

Grade Point Average

Safety School	Safety School	Attainable School	Reach School	Reach School
Subtract .3	Subtract .2	Your GPA	Add .2	Add .3

SAT Scores

Safety School	Safety School	Attainable School	Reach School	Reach School
Subtract 150 pts.	Subtract 100 pts.	Rdg. + Math	Add 100 pts.	Add 150 pts.

ACT Scores

Safety School	Safety School	Attainable School	Reach School	Reach School
Subtract 4 pts.	Subtract 3 pts.	Composite Score	Add 3 pts.	Add 4 pts.

COLLEGE SELECTION SURVEY

1. LOCATION

Distance, Geography and Environment

Take the college selection survey below: Circle your choices and write in your answers to start defining what you're looking for in a college.

Where do you want to live for the next four years in college?

Northeast:	ME	NH	VT	MA	CT	RI
	NY					
Mid-Atlantic:	PA	NJ	DE	MD	DC	
Southeast:	VA	WV	NC	SC	GA	FL
	AL	MS	TN	KY	AR	LA
Midwest:	ND	SD	NE	KS	MN	IW
	MO	WI	IL	MI	IN	OH
West:	ID	MT	WY	NV	UT	CO
	AZ					
West Coast:	WA	OR	CA			
Southwest:	NM	TX	OK	AZ		
Non-Contiguous:	AK	HI				

Environment:

Urban   Suburban   Small Town   Rural

How did you choose the states and environment?

_____

How often do you want to come home?

Every Weekend   1-2 times per month

Fall/Winter/Spring Break only

How far from home do you want to be?

Close   Far

Within 1 hour (50-60 miles)   1-2 hours (100-120 miles)

2-4 hours (120-240 miles)   Driving distance: 8-10 hours
(450-600 mi)

Distance does not matter

2. ACADEMICS

Academics, Majors, Student/Faculty Ratio, Special Education and Class Size

What kind of college would you like to attend?

Liberal Arts & Sciences   Engineering   Arts/Music

_____

_____

_____

What do you plan to study? On a scale of 1 to 10, how sure are you of your major?

_____

_____

_____

_____

Is it an absolute requirement that the college offer this major?

_____

_____

Are there any other class offerings that are must-haves? How hard do you want to work in college? (This criterion will be integral in your decision on the admissions rating—safety/attainable/reach)

_____

_____

Describe your ideal class (seminar, auditorium, in-between, lecture, interactive) (The size of the school will make a big difference here—the smaller the school or individual program, the more attention that you will receive from professors and the smaller the classes will be)

_____

_____

Average class size you would like:

Small (up to 20)   Medium (up to 35)   Large (Auditorium)

Will you be able to function in class sizes different from your preferences?

Yes   No

Will you consider a "safety school" with an honors program?

_____

_____

Will you need special education services in college, based on your Individualized Education Plan (IEP) or your Section 504 Plan?

Yes   No

3. SOCIAL LIFE

Size of the Student Body, Single Sex vs. Co-educational, Male/Female Ratio, Public vs. Private, Personality Fit, Campus Life, Greek Life and Housing

What size student body do you want?

Under 2,000   2,000 – 5,000   5000 – 10,000
10,000 – 20,000   20,000 +

Why did you pick this size student body?

_____

_____

Are you willing to consider and visit schools that are smaller or bigger than specified above? You will be amazed at what you learn!

      Yes   No

Will you consider a single-sex school? (Think about this before saying no—the single sex schools have a lot to offer including merit aid (huge scholarships!), lots of other colleges nearby, and great alumni networking.)

      Yes   No

Will you consider a military school or academy? (Some military schools do not require military service upon graduation)

      Yes   No

Will you consider public and/or private schools? (Don't discount all the merit aid that is available at private schools; many private schools are as affordable as public schools!)

      Public   Private

Different schools have very different cultures (liberal, conservative, socioeconomic—preppy/grunge/edgy, racial/religious/cultural mix). What type of campus environment would make you feel comfortable? Honestly, are you open to people who are different from you or do you feel best with people with backgrounds similar to yours? Think carefully about this issue and do not give a politically correct answer!

_____

_____

_____

_____

Do you want to attend a school with fraternities and sororities?

_____

_____

How important is school spirit to you? (Do you want lots of rah-rah football/basketball games and fun rivalries? Explain.)

_____

_____

_____

_____

How important are campus traditions to you? (Generally, the older and more established schools have more school traditions, like UVA's dressing up for football games or Longwood University's tradition of touching the statue of Joan of Arc. These traditions make students feel like they are part of a bigger whole. Explain your interest.)

_____

_____

_____

_____

How do you feel about partying? (Some campuses have really clamped down on partying, even expelling students for underage drinking. Some campuses are dry; they do not tolerate any alcohol use.)

_____

_____

Are religious organizations important to you? How do you feel about attending a religious-based school? (Although almost all private schools were founded by churches, many are religious in name only. Others like Grove City College, Liberty University and Oral Roberts University have significant religious curricula and requirements.)

_____

_____

_____

What type of housing would you prefer? (Most four-year colleges and universities offer on-campus housing. Make sure to see the campus housing when visiting. Dorms range from singles to triples to apartments to townhouses.)

Dormitory Apartment close to campus Commute from home

Do you want to have campus housing for all four years? (Many students choose to move off-campus by junior (third) year, as they become more mature and ready to venture into the adult world.)

    Yes   No

4. ACTIVITIES

Athletics and Activities

Do you want to play sports in college?

    Yes   No

At what level do you want to participate in these sports?

NCAA I NCAA II NCAA III
NAIA   Intramural/Club

What other activities are important to you? I have included spots for ten, but you don't have to have that many.

   1. _____

   2. _____

3. _____

4. _____

5. _____

6. _____

7. _____

8. _____

9. _____

10. _____

5. FINANCES

Will you need financial aid?

      Yes   No

Will you apply for scholarships/merit aid?

      Yes   No

Will you participate in Reserve Officer Training Corps?

      Yes   No

Which branch?

Army   Navy/Marine   Air Force

Is ROTC mandatory to your decision?

Yes   No

6. MORE

Is there anything else that you would like to mention?

_____

_____

_____

_____

_____

_____

_____

FANTASIZING

Now that you have completed the survey, indulge yourself with a little fantasy? Describe the perfect school for yourself. If you already have a few schools on your list, think about why they appeal to you.

_____

_____

_____

_____

_____

_____

_____

_____

PRELIMINARY LIST OF COLLEGES

Make a list of the colleges that you are considering:

1. _____   16. _____

2. _____   17. _____

3. _____   18. _____

4. _____   19. _____

5. _____   20. _____

6. _____   21. _____

7. _____   22. _____

8. _____   23. _____

9. _____   24. _____

10. _____   25. _____

11. _____

12. _____

13. _____

14. _____

15. _____

DEVELOPING YOUR VERY OWN COLLEGE LIST

There are several sample Professional Tutoring college selection spreadsheets for your review. The purpose of these spreadsheets is to lay out college options in black and white. You will notice that the spreadsheets, developed for our three students, Colin, Grace and Ally, are tailored to each student's wish lists.

Colin: Colin wanted a well-known school with a strong science curriculum to support his pre-medicine major. Colin's drive steered him toward schools that would help prepare him for medical school right after college. While Colin wanted to be within a reasonable distance of his mid-Atlantic home, he was open to looking at the midwest.

Grace: Grace had a tough time choosing between big universities with lots of school spirit and football games and smaller private colleges that would offer her personal attention in the classroom. Like Colin, Grace was considering a pre-med major. Unlike Colin, Grace wanted to participate in NCAA athletics (track and cheerleading). She also wanted a college with fraternities and sororities (listed under the "Greeks" column in her spreadsheet).

Ally: Ally had two NCAA Division III playing opportunities: soccer and lacrosse. She listed both in her spreadsheet as well as NCAA football (school spirit) and Greeks. For the most part, Ally wanted to be within several hours of her Washington, DC home. Ally also wanted to avoid commuter colleges (schools with little dorm space and a majority of students who live off-campus, especially at home).

Included with each College Selection Spreadsheet is the Admissions Probability Organizer for each student As you review the spreadsheets, remember each student's wish list and personality. Think about what you filled in on your survey and compare it to Colin, Grace, and Ally's college choices.

You will notice that some of the schools are highlighted and that some also have an X in the far left column. The highlights indicate good matches for Colin, Grace and Ally. The X indicates a probable application. By including about 30 schools on the list, students are able to develop a good college selection sample. It also helps to remind students and parents later that quite a few colleges were considered.

As you develop your own list, you will use your completed College Coaching Survey. You will use the 18 decision criteria listed earlier in the chapter and explored in your college selection survey. You may add columns to your spreadsheet as you need. Plan to include 15 to 30 possible colleges to your spreadsheet. Any more will become unmanageable.

If you have some colleges on your list, that is wonderful. If you do not have any idea of where to start, that is okay, also. Some good resources include:

1. Your school guidance counselor or career counselor;

2. Your teachers, current and former;

3. Your parents (yes, they have valuable opinions);

4. College Board's website; it has a feature called "College Matchmaker" that provides good help in narrowing options.

5. College guide books. My favorite is the annual *Barron's Guide to Colleges*. This great resource lists four-year universities in alphabetical order by state. Barron's sets itself apart by rating the universities by their admissions' selectivity. These ratings begin with "Most Competitive" and end with "Non-Competitive". The ratings will help you

determine your own selectivity indices of safety, attainability and reach.

Once you have developed your list, it will be time to begin online research and campus visits. By the very early part of your senior year, you should have the list narrowed to eight or nine schools.

Professional Tutoring recommends the following balance:

- Three Safety Schools
- Three Attainable Schools
- Two Reach Schools

Make sure that you give an equal amount of attention to all three ratings of schools and that you would happily attend any of the eight or nine schools on your list. This balancing will require more time and energy in research, visits, applications and interviews; and it is well worth the effort. Also remember, that it is the student who will spend four or more years at an individual college or university. Do not fall into the trap that I call the "Designer Shoe Syndrome." In the "Designer Shoe Syndrome," parents and students only want to consider the most selective or elite of schools, regardless of whether the college and student fit each other. They are much more interested in the name brand of the school than they are in the school itself. These parents and students lose sight of the student's needs and desires. A poor match pinches like a bad pair of shoes; the student will spend four years feeling out of place, academically and socially.

In addition, focusing on only the most selective schools (the reach schools) with only a minor glance at safety school alternatives will cause problems later in the senior year. All too often, seniors find themselves in the spring with only one or two acceptances from safety schools in which they have little or no interest. Some students find themselves without a single acceptance because they have "over-applied" (applied to only reach schools).

Several years ago in the middle of April, a distraught mother called me. When I answered the phone, I had a tough time even identifying who the caller was, as she was sobbing so hard. After several minutes, I finally figured out who was on the phone and made out the words, "the worst thing that could ever happen to our family has happened. It's Amy!" I fell backwards into a chair, tears welling in my eyes and my throat closing, for I was sure that Amy had died. What else could bring a mother to this point? Unfortunately, I had received such horrifying news previously in my educational career. Finally, through the sobs, Amy's mom choked out the distressing news, "Amy did not get into any of the ten colleges to which she applied!" I am not sure it helped when I answered, "Is that all?" Goodness, Amy was alive and well, and the worst that was going to happen was that Amy would spend a year at a community college.

Why was Amy's mother so distraught and how did this happen? Amy, a 4.0 student with a 750 Critical Reading, an 800 (perfect) Writing and a 590 Math SAT score had over-applied. An expensive, but less than competent, college coach had recommended that she apply to ten of our country's most elite colleges and universities including Harvard, Yale, Smith and the University of California. Amy's great grades and strong board scores did not guarantee her a slot at these universities. The coach seemed to gloss over the relatively weak math SAT score and set up Amy for major disappointment. The good news: Amy's mother and I immediately began to call other strong liberal arts colleges, just a step below elite, with Amy's student resume in-hand. Amy received offers from several fine schools. She even was offered significant merit money (scholarship).

Keep in mind, that the best match is often not the most selective school that will admit a student. Think about the unfortunate student who is accepted from the waiting list or by serious networking (arm-twisting) to a "top" university. This student may fall into the bottom ten percent of the university's class and will spend four years trying to keep up with the rest of the students. That is not a whole lot of fun, nor does it necessarily provide a good education, as the student scrambles to keep his/her head above water. It is hard to learn under these circumstances.

SAMPLE COLLEGE SELECTION SPREADSHEETS AND ADMISSIONS PROBABILITY WORKSHEETS

RATING SYSTEM	GOAL
White: Good Match	3 Safety
Gray: Better Match	3 Attainable
Gray with X: Best Match	2 Reach

STATS

Student	CR	Math	Total	Writing	Total	GPA
Colin	710	690	1400	560	1960	3.00
Grace	590	540	1130	670	1800	3.40
Allison	460	480	940	480	1420	2.60

COLIN McFIMIAN'S
Admissions Probability Organizer

Grade Point Average

Safety School	Safety School	Attainable School	Reach School	Reach School
Subtract .3	Subtract .2	3.10	Add .2	Add .3
2.80	2.90	3.10	3.30	3.40

SAT Scores

Safety School	Safety School	Attainable School	Reach School	Reach School
Subtract 150 pts.	Subtract 100 pts.	1960	Add 100 pts.	Add 150 pts.
1810	1860	1910 - 2010	2060	2110

ACT Scores

Safety School	Safety School	Attainable School	Reach School	Reach School
Subtract 4 pts.	Subtract 3 pts.	31	Add 3 pts.	Add 4 pts.
27	28	30-32	34	35

COLIN McFIMIAN'S College Selection Spreadsheet

	College	Location	Size	SAT-CR	SAT-Ma	Total	GPA	Rating
	California U. of PA	California, PA	6,299	493	493	986	3.10	S
	Virginia Commonwealth U.	Richmond, VA	21,260	550	570	1120	3.10	S
X	Purdue U.	West Lafayette, IN	30,424	545	590	1135	3.10	S
	Randolph-Macon U.	Ashland, VA	1,146	540	540	1080	3.20	S
	Temple U.	Philadelphia, PA	24,676	540	540	1080	3.20	S
X	U. Rhode Island	Kingston, RI	11,875	540	560	1100	3.20	S/A
X	East Carolina U.	Greenville, NC	16,835	550	570	1120	3.20	S
	Fairfield U.	Fairfield, CT	4,008	587	601	1188	3.20	S
	Goucher College	Towson, MD	1,300	620	570	1190	3.23	A
X	Drexel U.	Philadelphia, PA	11,011	585	610	1195	3.30	A
	Duquesne U.	Pittsburgh, PA	5,700	560	560	1120	3.40	A
	N.C State U.	Raleigh, NC	20,314	580	615	1195	3.40	A/R
	American University	Washington, DC	5,200	564	587	1151	3.42	A
	Washington College	Chestertown, MD	1,300	578	567	1145	3.44	A
	St. Joseph's U.	Philadelphia, PA	4,932	570	570	1140	3.50	A
	U. Delaware	Newark, DE	14,639	570	590	1160	3.50	a/r
	UMD-Baltimore County	Baltimore, MD	9,500	590	610	1200	3.50	A/R
	Providence College	Providence, RI	3,998	597	606	1203	3.50	A
	Drew U.	Madison, NJ	1,656	608	596	1204	3.50	A/R
X	Northeastern U.	Boston, MA	15,195	603	623	1226	3.50	A/R
X	Towson University	Towson, MD	13,300	555	535	1090	3.54	A
	George Washington U.	Washington, DC	10,000	620	620	1240	3.60	R
	U. of Mary Washington	Fredericksburg, VA	4,000	610	590	1200	3.66	A/R
X	U. of Pittsburgh	Pittsburgh, PA	15,367	592	600	1192	3.80	A/R
	Worcester Polytechnic I.	Worcester, MA	2,866	620	670	1290	3.80	R
X	Emory U.	Atlanta, GA	6,646	670	690	1360	3.80	R
X	Washington U. in Saint Louis	St. Louis, MO	7,386	710	740	1450	3.80	R

Costs	Pub/Private	Website	S/F Ratio	Sci Maj	Early A/D	Regular	Notification
$18,000.00	Public	cup.edu	20:01	11		Rolling	Rolling
$15,000.00	Public	vcu.edu		9	P-Feb 1	Rolling	Rolling-Nov 1
$30,000.00	Public	purdue.edu	15:01	28		Rolling	Rolling 9/15
$35,000.00	Private	rmc.edu	13:01	3	A&D	March 01	April 01
$19,000.00	Public	temple.edu	17:01	13		April 01	Rolling
$31,000.00	Public	uri.edu	15:01	15	A-Dec 15	February 01	Rolling
$25,000.00	Public	ecu.edu	17:01	19		Rolling	Rolling-10/1
$34,000.00	Private	fairfield.edu	17:01	4	A-Nov 15	January 15	April 01
$35,000.00	Private	goucher.edu	14:01	3	D-Dec 1	February 01	April 01
$40,000.00	Private	drexel.edu	14:01	16		March 01	April 01
$33,000.00	Private	duquesne.edu	12:01	9	A-Dec 1	Rolling	Rolling
$25,000.00	Public	ncsu.edu	19:01	12	A-Nov 1	February 01	April 01
$38,000.00	Private	american.edu	10:01	12	D-Nov 15	April 01	May 01
$35,000.00	Private	washcoll.edu	15:01	5	D-Nov 15	February 15	March 01
$31,000.00	Private	sju.edu	16:01	4		February 01	March 15
$26,000.00	Public	udel.edu	15:01	20		January 15	March 15
$24,000.00	Public	umbc.edu	17:01	14	check	May 15	Rolling
$40,000.00	Private	providence.edu	14:01	4	A-Nov 1	January 15	April 01
$45,000.00	Private	drew.edu	11:01	4	D-Dec 1	February 15	April 01
$43,000.00	Private	northeastern.edu	17:01	14	A-Nov 15	January 15	April 01
$25,000.00	Public	towson.edu	21:01	14		May 01	Rolling
$50,000.00	Private	gwu.edu	13:01	18	A/D-Nov 1	March 15	May 01
$15,000.00	Public	mwc.edu	17:01	4	D-Nov 1	February 01	April 01
$25,000.00	Public	pitt.edu	17:01	16		Rolling	Rolling-10/5
$45,000.00	Private	wpi.edu	13:01	9	A-Nov 15	February 01	April 01
$34,000.00	Private	emory.edu	6:01	5	D-Nov1	January 15	April 01
$37,000.00	Private	wustl.edu		12	D-Nov 15	January 15	April 01

COLIN McFIMIAN'S College Selection Spreadsheet (cont.)	
Comments	% Accepted
Cal. U of PA. Definite safety school	68%
VCU is definitely a safety school, associated with MCV	66%
Purdue is a nationally recognized program, Colin may quality for the honors program	79%
RMC would surely offer Colin scholarship $	58%
Temple is another Philly school, not necessarily my favorite but worth a look	60%
URI has fairly strong health program, ck local hospital and coop programs with Brown/Prov.	74%
East Carolina U. strong health sciences, check on hospital affiliations	77%
Fairfield U. is in a beautiful, suburban location	61%
(Goucher College) Towson is close to other schools, coop agreement with Hopkins	73%
Drexill U. has one of the best Co-op programs in the country, and highly recognized programs	76%
(Duquesne U.) Pittsburgh is a nice city, coop agreements between UPitt, Carnegie Mellon and Duquesne	72%
NCState is known for its science and engineering programs, great location in Raleigh, coops	57%
(American University) strong math/computer/sciences, nice size	69%
(Washington College) okay, so it is tiny, but Colin would get a lot of attention and it is a safety school	73%
(St. Joseph's U.) Very small science majors	47%
All my students love UDel, beautiful campus, strong programs	47%
(UMD-Baltimore) commuter campus?, check campus life, but Baltimore is a neat place for college	66%
Providence is a beautiful school, may have coop program with Brown and URI	48%
Drew is a very nice school in NJ, about 20 minutes from NYC in horse country	64%
Northeastern is in a great location, lots of science and health majors	45%
(Towson University) Towson has a huge health program, definitely a good match	59%
(George Washington U.) strong science majors, affiliation with hospital	39%
UMW is a bit of a wild card, but Colin is a male with strong math & science	55%
U Pitt is a beautiful school, I think that this would be a really good match for Colin	54%
(Worcester Polytechnic I.) Mostly male dominated school, has pre-med and strong sciences	67%
Emory is a little bastion of NY in the south, well known and respected	32%
(Washington U. in St. Louis) check with Wash U about policy with Early decision	21%

GRACE BENNINGTON
Admissions Probability Organizer

Grade Point Average

Safety School	Safety School	Attainable School	Reach School	Reach School
Subract .3	Subtract .2	3.40	Add .2	Add .3
3.10	3.20	3.40	3.60	3.70

SAT Scores

Safety School	Safety School	Attainable School	Reach School	Reach School
Subtract 150 pts.	Subtract 100 pts.	1130	Add 100 pts.	Add 150 pts.
980	1030	1080-1180	1230	1280

ACT Scores

Safety School	Safety School	Attainable School	Reach School	Reach School
Subtract 4 pts.	Subtract 3 pts.	27	Add 3 pts.	Add 4 pts.
23	24	26-28	30	31

GRACE BENNINGTON'S College Selection Spreadsheet

	College	Location	Size	SAT-CR	SAT-Ma	Total	GPA	Rating
	California U. of Pennsylvania	California, PA	7,000	493	493	986	3.00	S
X	High Point U.	High Point, NC	2,750	510	500	1010	3.00	S
X	Lynchburg College	Lynchburg, VA	2,213	510	510	1020	3.10	S
X	Radford U.	Radford, VA	8,155	516	539	1055	3.10	S
	East Carolina U.	Greenville, NC	16,835	495	515	1010	3.20	S
	West Virginia U.	Morgantown, WV	15,181	512	521	1033	3.20	S
X	Longwood U.	Farmville, VA	3,700	530	535	1065	3.20	S
	Randolph-Macon College	Ashland, VA	1,176	535	545	1080	3.20	S
	Coastal Carolina U.	Conway, SC	7,100	504	516	1020	3.25	S
X	Meredith College	Raleigh-Durham, NC	2,039	500	520	1020	3.30	S
	Drexel U.	Philadelphia, PA	11,011	585	610	1195	3.30	A
X	Christopher Newport U.	Newport News, VA	5,192	575	600	1175	3.35	A
X	Roanoke College	Salem, VA	2,006	550	545	1095	3.40	A
X	Duquesne U.	Pittsburgh, PA	5,700	560	560	1120	3.40	A
	U. South Carolina	Columbia, SC	18,648	570	590	1160	3.40	A
	Drew U.	Madison, NJ	1,666	585	580	1165	3.40	A
	Providence College	Providence, RI	4,000	580	590	1170	3.40	A/R
	UNC-Charlotte	Charlotte, NC	11,340	520	530	1050	3.50	A
	Hollins U.	Roanoke, VA	1,100	585	525	1110	3.50	A
	Sweet Briar College	Sweet Briar, VA	800	565	545	1110	3.50	S
	Fairfield U.	Fairfield, CT	4,000	575	595	1170	3.50	A/R
	U. Mary Washington	Fredericksburg, VA	4,000	610	580	1190	3.50	A/R
X	Clemson U.	Clemson, SC	14,270	600	625	1225	3.54	R
	UNC-Wilmington	Wilmington, NC	10,753	560	574	1134	3.60	A
	Elon U.	Elon, NC	5,000	600	610	1210	3.60	R
X	James Madison U.	Harrisonburg, VA	15,000	560	560	1120	3.62	R
	Va Tech	Blacksburg, VA	23,000	600	600	1200	3.70	R

GRACE BENNINGTON'S College Selection Spreadsheet (cont.)

Costs	Track	Cheer	Greeks	Public/Private	Website	S/F Ratio	M/F Ratio	Retention
$19,000.00	extensive	Club	X	Public	cup.edu	20:01	50/50	79%
$30,000.00	IColl	IColl	X	Private	highpoint.edu	19:01	38/62	79%
$35,000.00	DIII	DIII	X	Private	lynchburg.edu	14:01	46/54	73%
$15,000.00	IColl	IColl	X	Public	radford.edu	21:01	40/60	77%
$25,000.00	Club	Club	X	Public	ecu.edu	17:01	41/59	77%
$25,000.00	IColl	Club	X	Public	arc.wvu.edu	14:01	54/46	79%
$15,000.00	XC	Club	X	Public	longwood.edu	21:01	34/66	79%
$37,000.00		Club	X	Private	rmc.edu	13:01	47/53	72%
$28,000.00	IColl	IColl	X	Public	coastal.edu	25:01	46/54	71%
$30,000.00	XC			Private	meredith.edu	13:01	0/100	74%
$40,000.00	Club		X	Private	drexel.edu	14:01	60/40	
$15,000.00	DIII	DIII	X	Public	cnu.edu	22:01	39/61	82%
$37,250.00	DIII	DIII	X	Private	roanoke.edu	14:01	41/59	74%
$33,000.00	Club	Club	X	Private	duquesne.edu	12:01	40/60	88%
$28,000.00	IColl	IColl	X	Private	usc.edu	17:01	43/57	87%
$47,000.00	XC III	Club		Private	drew.edu	11:01	40/60	81%
$43,000.00	IColl			Private	providence.edu	14:01	44/56	92%
$25,000.00	IColl	IColl	X	Public	uncc.edu	19:01	46/54	77%
$37,000.00				Private	hollins.edu	12:01	0/100	68%
$38,000.00				Private	sbc.edu	10:01	0/100	75%
$47,000.00	Imural			Private	fairfield.edu	17:01	41/59	88%
$15,000.00	DIII	DIII		Public	umw.edu	17:01	32/68	87%
$28,000.00	DI	DI	X	Public	clemson.edu	14:01	52/48	89%
$22,000.00	IColl	IColl	X	Public	uncw.edu	19:01	41/59	85%
$32,000.00	Club	Club	X	Private	elon.edu	17:01	42/58	90%
$15,000.00	Club	Club	X	Public	jmu.edu	21:01	39/61	91%
$15,000.00	DI	DI	X	Public	vt.edu	17:01	50/50	93%

GRACE BENNINGTON'S College Selection Spreadsheet (cont.)

% Accepted	Early A/D	Regular	Notification	Comments
64%	n/a	Rolling	Rolling	CUP would be a major safety school for GB, cheer, gymnastics, Merit $$
73%	D-Nov 3	March 14	Rolling	HPoint has Ed & CJ, very preppy, MB would surely qualify for merit $
69%	D-Nov 15	Rolling	Rolling	Mrs. Ross loved Lynchburg, Grace could run/cheer, get in touch with Gigi
78%	A-Dec 15	Feb. 01	March 20	Radford would be a major safety, check out honors programs, GB likes hot guys there, gymnastics
77%		March 15	Rolling 10/1	Lots of opportunities and school spirit, in state tuition??
94%		August 01	Rolling	Mountaineers, good safety, large school with lots of opportunities
78%	D-Dec 1	March 01	Rolling	Longwood is not a bad in-state choice but I think that GB will have lots of others
61%	A-Nov 15	Feb. 01	April 01	RMC would be a safety school for GB, no track, cheer club
68%	n/a	Rolling	Rolling	Beautiful school, check on in-state tuition
88%	D-Oct 15	Rolling	Rolling	This is a WC worth looking at b/c of location
76%		March 01	April 01	One of the best Co-op programs in the country, and highly recognized, Merit $$
54%	A-Dec 1	Rolling	Rolling	CNU is a newer school, becoming a reach school for many kids. check out Leadership Program!!
73%	D-Dec 1	March 01	Rolling	Grace really liked Roanoke at visit, may be able to run/cheer
72%	A-Dec	Rolling	Rolling	Mrs. Ross loves Pittsburgh, coop agreements with UPitt, Carnegie-Melon, great opportunities
63%	D-Dec 1	Dec. 01	Rolling	Everone loves USC, fairly large school
77%	D-Dec 1	Feb.	Rolling	Very, very expensive
41%	A-Nov 1	Jan.15	April 01	No frats, no cheer/ low running
70%	A-Oct 15	July 01	Rolling	interesting possibility, Charlotte is not too far from Duke, Wake, UNC-Chapel Hill
88%	D-Dec 1	Feb. 01	Rolling	Grace liked Hollins a lot at the visit, but not sure of woman's college
81%	D-Dec 1	Feb. 01	March 15	SBC is beautiful and has an amazing riding program
55%	A-Nov 15	Jan. 15	April 01	Fairfield has a beautiful campus near family
80%	A-Jan 15	Feb. 01	April 01	UMW is a good school to consider, has riding, high female ratio
50%	n/a	Dec. 01	Rolling	Clemson is a beautiful school, definitely a reach
58%	A-Nov 1	Feb. 01	April 01	UNC Wilmington might be a really good match, nice size
41%	D-Nov 1	Jan. 10	March 15	Elon is a very expensive reach school
64%		Jan. 15		JMU is one of G's top choices, bit of a reach and a big school
67%	D-Nov 1	Jan. 15	April 01	VaTech is a really neat school, but probably too big for MB right out of high school

ALLISON LEIGH
Admissions Probability Organizer

Grade Point Average

Safety School	Safety School	Attainable School	Reach School	Reach School
Subtract .3	Subtract .2	2.60	Add .2	Add .3
2.30	2.40	2.60	2.80	2.90

SAT Scores

Safety School	Safety School	Attainable School	Reach School	Reach School
Subtract 150 pts.	Subtract 100 pts.	940	Add 100 pts.	Add 150 pts.
790	840	940	1040	1090

ACT Scores

Safety School	Safety School	Attainable School	Reach School	Reach School
Subtract 4 pts.	Subtract 3 pts.	20	Add 3 pts.	Add 4 pts.
16	17	19-21	23	24

ALLISON LEIGH'S College Selection Spreadsheet

	College	Location	Size	SAT-CR	SAT-Ma	Total	GPA	Rating
	Mt. Aloysius	Cresson, PA	1,520	460	455	915	2.00	S
X	Ferrum College	Ferrum, VA	1,060	452	470	922	2.64	S
	Peace College	Raleigh, NC	702	470	460	930	2.90	S
	Mount Olive College	Mount Olive, NC	2,700	460	470	930	3.00	S
	Concord U.	Athens, WV	2,823	475	465	940	3.60	A
	University of North Carolina-Pembrooke	Pembrooke, NC	5,237	465	480	945	3.00	S
X	University of Virginia - Wise	Wise, VA	1,911	475	480	955	2.50	S
X	Frostburg U.	Frostburg, MD	4,252	480	485	965	3.00	A
X	Greensboro College	Greensboro, NC	1,145	490	485	975	2.50	S
	Brevard College	Brevard, NC	598	494	484	978	3.00	A
	Bethany College	Bethany, WV	833	490	495	985	3.45	A
X	California U. of Pennsylvania	California, PA	7,000	493	493	986	3.00	A
	Lander University	Greenwood, SC	2,568	491	501	992	3.50	A
	Marymount U.	Arlington, VA	2,238	510	490	1000	3.00	A
	St. Andrew's Presbyterian College	Laurinburg, NC	693	500	500	1000	3.00	R
X	Slippery Rock U.	Slippery Rock, PA	7,100	500	500	1000	3.00	A
	Marshall U.	Huntington, WV	8,000	510	500	1010	3.10	A
	Anderson U.	Anderson, SC	1,874	495	515	1010	3.50	A
	Middle Tennessee U.	Murfreesboro, TN	20,643	515	505	1020	2.96	A/R
X	Radford U.	Radford, VA	8,155	510	510	1020	3.10	A
X	High Point University	High Point, NC	2,657	510	515	1025	2.80	A
X	Lynchburg College	Lynchburg, VA	1,600	518	508	1026	3.10	A
	Coastal Carolina U.	Conway, SC	7,070	510	520	1030	2.90	A
X	West Virginia U.	Morgantown, WV	18,000	512	521	1033	3.20	A
X	East Carolina University	Greenville, NC	16,835	515	525	1040	3.06	R
	Old Dominion U.	Norfolk, VA	15,464	520	521	1041	3.10	R
	Bridgewater College	Bridgewater, VA	1,541	520	530	1050	3.20	R
	Lenoir-Rhyne College	Hickory, NC	1,322	522	543	1065	3.00	R
	Virginia Commonwealth U.	Richmond, VA	6,880	535	535	1070	3.10	A
X	Longwood U.	Farmville, VA	3,440	530	550	1080	3.30	R

ALLISON LEIGH'S College Selection Spreadsheet (cont.)

Football	LAX	Soccer	Greeks	Costs	Public/Private	Website	% Accepted
no	no	DIII	no	$24,000.00	Private	mtaloy.edu	72%
DIII	DIII	DIII	check	$28,000.00	Private	ferrum.edu	91%
no	no	DIII	no	$30,000.00	Private	peace.edu	75%
no	no	DII	no	$18,500.00	Private	mountolivecollege.edu	n/a
DII	no	DII	yes	$16,000.00	Public	concord.edu	69%
DII	no	DII	yes	$19,000.00	Public	uncp.edu	86%
InterCol	no	no	yes	$15,000.00	Public	uvawise.edu	81%
DIII	DIII	DIII	yes	$22,000.00	Public	frostburg.edu	70%
DIII	DIII	DIII	yes	$29,000.00	Private	gborocollege.edu	74%
DII	no	DII	no	$28,000.00	Private	brevard.edu	82%
DIII	no	DIII	yes	$26,000.00	Private	bethanywv.edu	63%
InterColl	IntraMural	DIII	yes	$19,000.00	Public	cup.edu	79%
no	DII	DII	yes	$20,000.00	Public	lander.edu	81%
no	DIII	DIII	no	$32,000.00	Private	marymount.edu	81%
no	DII	DII	no	$26,000.00	Private	sapc.edu	84%
DII	DII	DII	yes	$17,000.00	Public	sru.edu	70%
DIA	no	DI	yes	$19,000.00	Public	marshall.edu	86%
no	no	DII	no	$25,000.00	Private	andersonuniversity.edu	85%
DIA	club	DI	yes	$23,000.00	Public	mtsu.edu	57%
no	no	DI	yes	$15,000.00	Public	radford.edu	78%
no	Club	DI	yes	$28,000.00	Private	highpoint.edu	87%
no	DIII	DIII	yes	$35,000.00	Private	lynchburg.edu	75%
DIAA	no	DI	yes	$25,000.00	Public	coastal.edu	68%
DI	club	DI	yes	$28,000.00	Public	arc.wvu	94%
DIA	club	DI	yes	$21,000.00	Public	ecu.edu	77%
no	DI	DI	yes	$15,000.00	Public	odu.edu	69%
DIII	DIII	DIII	no	$32,000.00	Private	bridgewater.edu	84%
DII	no	DII	yes	$31,000.00	Private	lrc.edu	81%
no	club	DI	yes	$15,000.00	Public	vcu.edu	66%
no	DI	DI	yes	$15,000.00	Public	longwood.edu	78%

ALLISON LEIGH'S College Selection Spreadsheet (cont.)

Comments	Early A/D	Regular	Notification
Commuter school but safety		Rolling	Rolling
Safety, not too far from home, but might be a bit too country		March 01	Rolling
Very small school		Rolling	Rolling
Near Wilmington, small school, no Greeks commuter school, has sports		Rolling	Rolling
Nice school, out of state but not too expensive, has arts major		Rolling	Rolling
Ally may be able to play soccer here, a bit of a commuter school, close to VA tuition		Rolling	Rolling
I suspect that UVA Wise will be an up and coming school soon		December 01	Rolling
Nice size, not too far away, has all 3 sports and Greeks		Rolling	Rolling
Nice school, possibly safety, to consider		December 15	Rolling
Very small, but nice S/F and M/F ratio		Rolling	2/15 +
Large arts program, worth a look		April 01	Rolling
CUP is a nice size, price similar to Va - take a look	n/a	Rolling	Rolling
Open admissions policy - this one is pretty much guaranteed		Rolling	Rolling
Marymount is very close to home, worth a quick visit	n/a	Rolling	Rolling
SAPC is similar to High Point, small, private, preppy		May 01	Rolling after 4/1
SRU has a lot of what Ally wants and is not real expensive, take a look		Rolling	Rolling
Marshall is also a nice size		Rolling	Rolling
Anderson may be a religious school - check on line	n/a	Rolling	Rolling
Worth a look, well known in its geographic area, has some of the attributes Ally wants		Rolling	Rolling
Radford is a nice size, only has soccer		February 01	Rolling
High Point has major, Greeks, is very preppy, small		Rolling	Rolling
Mrs. Ross likes Lynchburg, quiet in the country, interview	D-Nov 15	Rolling	Rolling
Coastal is a nice school near Myrtle Beach, Ally should contact the coach	n/a	Rolling	Rolling
large public university, has Mountaineers sports and major, worth a look	yes	August 01	Rolling
ECU is a nice school to consider, large univ. opportunities		Rolling	Rolling
ODU is in the city, not very pretty school, does not have his major		March 15	Rolling
BC is close to JMU so good location, may be a reach school		Rolling	Rolling
LRC is a beautiful school, has fraternities, traditions		Rolling	Rolling
VCU is a great size, a bit gritty in the city but has major		February 01	Rolling
Longwood is a reach, take a tour and submit application BY AUGUST 15 THIS YEAR!!!!!	D-Dec 1	March 01	Rolling

The Numbers Game: Statistical Qualifications

· ·

Now that you have developed a list of possible colleges and universities, it is time to play the numbers game. Because most colleges and universities do not have time to really get to know individual students in all their facets, the admissions process relies heavily on two all-important numbers: the Grade Point Average and the Board Scores (SAT Reasoning Exam and ACT Exam). In general, these two numbers are more important than anything else in the college admissions offices' initial evaluation of an applicant. And yes, admissions officers do understand that some schools offer inherently more rigorous curricula and different grading scales. While most schools grade on the ten-point scale (90-100 = A), some do not. Other school systems have fought grade inflation by changing the scale to a 94-100 for an A. One Virginia school system counts 94-100 as an A with a 93 equaling a B, not even a B+! Thus, the great equalizer, standardized tests, enters the equation. Fortunately, most schools will use the highest scores from separate sittings. For example, State University may use a student's

May Critical Reading Score and June Math Score to have the highest possible total. While extracurricular activities, good application essays, work experience and recommendations will be considered, the exam scores and the GPA really open the door to the admissions offices. To help understand the impact of the scores and grades, the next page includes a sample chart of average and minimum GPA, SAT Reasoning Exam Scores (Critical Reading and Math scores combined) and ACT scores for the Virginia public schools. If your school does not offer this data, consider helping your guidance office to develop such a spreadsheet. Many school systems offer similar information online through software such as Naviance. This type of chart will help in developing admissions ratings (safety, attainable and reach) for your individual case. Remember that, in general, the schools will fall into the following categories:

SAFETY

The students' exam scores and grade point average (GPA) will both be above the average statistics listed and significantly higher than the minimums listed. In order for a college to qualify as a safety school, its average or median SAT scores (Critical Reading and Math scores only) for accepted students should be at least 100-150 points below the prospective student's scores. The ACT will be three to four points below your score. In addition, the average or median GPA should be at least two to three tenths of a point below the prospective student's GPA. Remember that you will have the greatest probability of securing merit scholarships from safety schools.

ATTAINABLE

The students' exam scores and GPA will be on par with the average statistics listed and higher than the minimums listed. What does "on par" mean? This means that the average or median SAT scores (Critical Reading and Math, only) for accepted students at the target college or university will be within 50 to 70 points of the prospective student's SAT scores and within one to two points of the school's median ACT. The average GPA will be within one to two tenths of a point of the prospective student's. In the best case scenario, if the prospective student's SAT scores are slightly below the target university's averages, the student's GPA will be slightly above, thereby balancing the slightly lower SAT score or vice versa.

REACH

Either the students' exam scores and/or GPA are below the average statistics listed but as high as or higher than the minimums listed. A reasonable reach school will have SAT scores within approximately 100-150 points (for Critical Reading and Math sum) of the average accepted student. The ACT scores will be a maximum of four points beneath the prospective school's median ACT scores for admitted students and the school's reported average GPA will fall within .2 to .3 points of the interested student's GPA. If the university's exam scores and the GPA are both above these markers, and the student has no other major "hook" (athletics/disability/major recommendation), the college is most likely out of reach.

Professional Tutoring Philosophy: In the College Coaching Process, Professional Tutoring recommends that students apply to eight colleges/universities: three safety, three attainable and two reach schools. At the same time, more schools may be added, as long as this distribution is followed. Remember Amy's story. You do not want to land in the spring of your senior year with few or no college admissions!

ADMISSIONS STATISTICS
FOR 2007—VIRGINIA PUBLIC UNIVERSITIES

Below are the statistics for students from the Robinson Secondary School, Fairfax, VA (class of 2007) who were accepted at the following public Virginia Universities. Use this as a template, to fill in (with numbers), the schools you're considering.

Virginia Public Universities	GPA Avg.	GPA Min.	SAT Avg.	SAT Min.	ACT Avg.	ACT Min.	% Admit.
Virginia State University	2.81	2.55	845	820	15	15	50%
Radford University	3.12	2.24	1063	840	22	17	80%
Old Dominion University	3.07	2.43	1064	870	21	16	82%
Longwood University	3.22	2.83	1096	940	22	16	72%
University of Virginia-Wise	2.91	2.71	1120	910	n/a	n/a	50%
Virginia Commonwealth University	3.19	2.13	1120	870	22	16	81%
James Madison University	3.62	3.14	1120	960	26	21	56%
Christopher Newport University	3.36	2.66	1148	840	23	17	67%
George Mason University	3.46	2.72	1155	840	24	17	66%
University of Mary Washington	3.51	2.83	1207	950	24	18	80%
Virginia Military Institute	3.31	3.14	1247	1070	n/a	n/a	60%
Virginia Polytechnic Institute (VA Tech)	3.71	2.94	1267	1000	27	22	58%
University of Virginia	3.93	3.20	1341	1080	29	26	40%
College of William and Mary	3.95	3.57	1370	1220	29	26	37%

THE EXAMS: SAT REASONING EXAM VS. ACT EXAM DECISION CRITERIA

Have you heard the rumor that the ACT College Entrance Exam is so much easier than the SAT Reasoning Exam? Well, that is definitely just a rumor. While the ACT is more widely accepted nationally, the SAT Reasoning Exam is the preferred exam east of the Mississippi River. Many colleges will accept either or both exams.

Both the ACT and the SAT exams attempt to measure students' preparedness for university-level work. Since grades are not equivalent across schools, districts, regions and states, the colleges must have some type of measurement to compare students. Thus, the two major entrance exams have found a niche. The differences are outlined below.

The ACT is made up of four subject areas: English, Math, Reading and Science. The exam administration requires a total of 205 minutes, almost three and a half hours. The English section includes 75 questions covering grammar, language/word usage and rhetorical skills (writing and editing). This section is 45 minutes long. The Math section covers math areas from seventh through twelfth grades (Pre-algebra, Algebra I and II, Geometry and Trigonometry). This 60-minute section covers 60 math problems. The Reading section has 40 questions and takes 35 minutes. It requires reading comprehension skills. The Science section is 35 minutes long and includes 40 questions covering Biology, Chemistry and Earth Science. The last section, the essay, is optional, but I highly recommend it; the top schools require this section. This section provides the students with a prompt and 30 minutes to write a college essay. The ACT does not penalize a student for wrong answers. The ACT Assessment receives a score from one to 36 points.

To prepare for the ACT Assessment, Professional Tutoring recommends *The Real ACT Prep Guide*, published by Thomson/Peterson's (ISBN: 0-7689-1975-4, cover price: $19.95). For vocabulary review, nothing is better than consistent reading at grade level, e.g., the *Harry Potter* series, or *The Hot Zone*. In The Professional Tutoring SAT Preparation Courses, I use several vocabulary books and require the students to memorize lists (very boring, but effective).

Although, rumored to be much more difficult than the ACT exam, the SAT Reasoning exam is similar to the ACT. This 235 minute exam is 30 minutes longer than the ACT. It is divided into three subject areas: Critical Reading, Math and Writing. The Critical Reading section is divided into three sub-sections, two of 25 minutes and one of 20 minutes. It includes sentence completions (multiple-choice, fill-in-the-blank) and short reading passages (one to two paragraphs) and long reading passages (full page). As in the ACT's Reading Section, the SAT tests students' ability to read and understand college-level material, including advanced vocabulary. The Math section will also include three sections with the same time break-down. Like the ACT, the SAT will test students' knowledge of high school level math. Although, the SAT is likely to have more complex math questions than the ACT, the exams require similar math skills. In addition, the ACT tests on basic trigonometry including triangle and sine and cosine curves. In contrast, the SAT does not test on trigonometry, other than the two basic triangles (30-60-90 and 45-45-90). The third section of the SAT is the Writing Section. The Writing section totals 60 minutes, including two 25-minute sections and one ten-minute section. The SAT always opens with the required 25-minute essay. Like the ACT, the SAT provides a written prompt and asks students to respond. The second two writing sections test grammar, word usage and editing skills. In addition, the SAT I will include one experimental section (Critical Reading, Math or Writing) which the College Board uses in developing new tests. This 25-minute "wild card" section is not graded; it is also not identified to the students. In contrast to the ACT Assessment, the SAT Reasoning Exam alternates the ten sections; each individual SAT section is shorter than the ACT's sections. The SAT penalizes students one quarter of a point for each incorrect answer. At this point, most schools afford the Critical Reading and Math scores the greatest weight. Most schools do not give much, if any, consideration to the "new" writing section.

Each section of the SAT is scored individually. The lowest score is 200 points and the highest is 800 points. When added together, the three scores will total between 600 and 2400 points. The statistical median is 1500 total points. Many colleges consider 1500 a minimum score for admission and 1800 the mark for honors programs or academic scholarships. To prepare for the SAT Reasoning exam, Professional Tutoring has developed an approximate 150-page workbook tailored to the curriculum established in 2005. In addition, the College Board's *Official SAT Study Guide for the New SAT* (ISBN: 0-87447-718-2, cover price: $19.95) is an excellent resource (The College Board is due to release a second edition in 2009).

The ACT does not penalize students for incorrect answers and the SAT Reasoning Exam deducts one quarter of a point for all wrong answers. Both tests are scored on the basis of the number of questions answered correctly. Omitting questions to avoid the one quarter SAT penalty may ultimately harm students, as the student will earn fewer points toward his/her score.

SAT VS ACT SCORING SPREADSHEET

ACT SCORE	SAT SCORE: Critical Reading + Math	SAT SCORE: Critical Reading, Math + Writing
36	1600	2400
35	1580	2340
34	1530	2260
33	1480	2190
32	1430	2130
31	1380	2040
30	1340	1980
29	1300	1920
28	1260	1860
27	1220	1820
26	1180	1760
25	1140	1700
24	1100	1650
23	1070	1590
22	1030	1530
21	1000	1500
20	960	1410
19	910	1350
18	870	1290
17	830	1210
16	780	1140
15	730	1060
14	680	1000
13	620	900
12	560	780
11	500	750

THE MONTHS THAT THE SAT AND ACT EXAMS ARE OFFERED

I recommend that you verify the following dates online at CollegeBoard.com and act.org

SAT Reasoning Exams: October, November, December, January, March or April, May, June

SAT Subject Exams: October, November, December, January, May, June

ACT Exam: September (limited states/locations), October, December, February, April, June

SITTING FOR THE SAT/ACT EXAMS

Generally, students take the SAT Reasoning and/or the ACT exams one or two times during their junior year and once during their senior year. Some parents and students think that it is a good idea to get a jump on these tests by freshman year. I do not find that taking the formal exams early help students at all. In contrast, I have found over the years, that repeated testing leads to burn-out and stressed-out students. If you want to have an idea of future scores, rely on your PSAT scores and/or take timed practice exams at home or in a structured class.

REGISTERING FOR THE SAT AND ACT EXAMS

To register for the SAT Reasoning Exam or SAT Subject Tests, log on to CollegeBoard.org. To register for the ACT exam, log on to ACT.org. Plan to spend 30 minutes online. This can be a laborious process which requires both the student and the parent. The sites also require a credit card number to register.

Both the College Board and the ACT Corporation will send scores to up to four colleges/universities at no cost. In order to take advantage of the four free score reports, you need to register for the four colleges to receive your scores within days of the actual test day. If you register for your scores to be sent to the colleges at this time, the College Board and the ACT Inc. will send your scores at the same time that they notify you of the results. If you want to review the scores before sending them to the colleges, DO NOT specify your colleges at the time of registration.

REPORTING THE SCORES

As of the spring of 2009, both the College Board and the ACT, Inc., will allow students to choose which scores from specific test dates to send to colleges. What does this mean? It means that a student who has taken the SAT or ACT several times may choose to send the results from one or two specific test dates as opposed to scores from all of a student's test dates. In order to take advantage of this new perk, students give up the four free reports offered at registration. It is well worth the nominal fee (approximately $9 per college) to wait for results.

DISABILITY ACCOMMODATIONS

Students who have a current Individualized Education Plan (IEP) or a 504 Plan may be eligible for testing accommodations, such as additional testing time, bubbling support, or a reader. Approval for accommodations must be requested through the College Board and the ACT and the approval number must be provided by the parent/student at registration. The student's school case manager or special education department will help with this process. Applying for accommodations on either test is not a simple process. Plan to start at least six months before your test date.

FEE WAIVERS

Both the College Board and the ACT Corporation will waive fees upon request with the appropriate low income documentation. The processes for both exams are similar:

1. Guidance Counselors have the authority to approve a fee waiver.

2. Generally to qualify, your family income must be near the guidelines for the Federal Free and Reduced Lunch/National School LunchProgram.

3. The final decision is left to the guidance counselor's discretion.

4. Juniors and Seniors only are eligible for the SAT Reasoning Exam and ACT waivers.

5. Freshmen and Sophomores may apply for fee waivers for the SAT Subject exams.

Remember that these are general guidelines. For more information, make sure to check the College Board and ACT websites (CollegeBoard.com, ACT.org).

PREPARING FOR THE SAT AND/OR ACT EXAMS

Stories abound of students who take the SAT Reasoning or ACT exams with no preparation whatsoever and earn a perfect score. These stories are urban legends! Both the SAT Reasoning and the ACT Exams are standardized tests designed to rank students according to knowledge and skill levels. Whatever you do, do not take these tests cold, even for a baseline exam.

So how do you prepare? There are quite a few options ranging from home study to classes to individual tutoring. Which option is best? It, of course, depends on your individual level of motivation, budget and goals.

The home study options include working through a test preparation book, forming a study group or registering for an online class. Classes will range from very short (a weekend) to long (nine months or more). Individual tutoring may cost $75 or more per hour. I have heard of tutors charging several hundred dollars per hour for customized work.

Regardless, before choosing a preparation plan, do your research. Some questions to ask include:

1. What are the instructors' qualifications?

2. How much training do the instructors undergo before being allowed to enter the classroom?

3. Are all instructors certified teachers or do they all at least hold four-year college degrees?

4. Does one instructor cover all three facets of the SAT (Critical Reading, Math and Writing)?

5. Does a single instructor cover all four subject areas of the ACT (Reading, Writing, Math and Science)?

6. Does the organization guarantee the same instructor(s) for the duration of the course? (One Professional Tutoring student bailed out of a six-week SAT preparation class after the third week because the class had different substitutes for each of the bi-weekly sessions).

7. Is there a score guarantee?

8. What are the requirements to earn the right to the score guarantee?

9. What are the terms of the score guarantee? Many test preparation companies guarantee an improvement of 100-150 points. Few offer a money-back guarantee. Most offer the opportunity to repeat the course IF the student has completed all homework and attended class. If the course does not work for you, will you want to take the same curriculum again? Remember that you have a limited time to do well on these exams – you must be finished by the winter of your senior year.

10. What happens if the test preparation company has issues such as teacher turn over?

11. What curriculum does the test preparation company use?

12. How many full-length exams does the course include? This is tricky because students do need to practice taking exams BUT

some companies test during more than half the class time to avoid the instructors having to teach.

13. Does the test preparation company divide the students by skill level?

14. Is the class a specific length or do students cycle through as needed?

15. Are make-up classes offered for absences?

16. What happens in the case of extreme family situations/emergencies?

17. Finally, ask for references of satisfied customers.

SAT—SUBJECT TESTS

Less well-known than the SAT Reasoning Exam are the SAT Subject Exams, formerly called the SAT II Exams. These one-hour exams measure students' knowledge of specific academic areas. Generally, only the most selective (Ivy League) colleges require that students take three SAT Subject exams. Other elite schools recommend, but do not require, two to three SAT Subject Exams. Some schools use the data for admissions and others for placement. Check the individual college websites for requirements.

While the SAT Reasoning Exam tests both knowledge and reasoning skills, the SAT subject tests truly evaluate in-depth knowledge of the specific subject areas. As the SAT Subject Exams are only one hour in length, students may register for up to three exams in one sitting. The SAT Subject exams are given at the same time and locations as the SAT Reasoning Exams.

Current SAT II Subject Exams

Literature	French
U.S. History	German
World History	Chinese
Math I	Italian
Math II	Japanese
Chemistry	Korean
Biology E/M	Latin
Physics	Modern Hebrew
Spanish	

Dates Offered: October, November, December, January, May, June (not offered in March/April)

Professional Tutoring Recommendations

Although many counselors recommend that students take the subject exams immediately following the completion of a course, e.g. Subject II – Biology, immediately after finishing freshman biology, Professional Tutoring students have found the SAT II Subject exams much more difficult and comprehensive than the average high school curriculum. Most students perform best on these exams after completing the appropriate Advanced Placement (AP) or International Baccalaureate (IB) course. Nevertheless, my students also find that they must study six to eight hours even after completing the comparable AP or IB exam. Do not take these tests lightly!

Professional Tutoring Students have reported that they have found two exams at a single sitting reasonable. The third exam often is too much at one time. These tests are not a slam-dunk. They are difficult and require studying and review. Most students report success with six to eight hours of preparation for each individual exam.

TEST DAY ADVICE

Over 15 years of preparing students to take the SAT and ACT exams, Professional Tutoring has developed a list of test day tips. Seriously, some of these tips may seem silly to you BUT they can make or break your SAT/ACT exam! Trust me; I am old with lots of experience in helping students through this process.

1. Register to take the SAT/ACT Exam at your local school, if offered. You will feel much more comfortable in your own environment.

2. If you are not able to register for your base school, parents should plan on driving their child to the test center. When a student gets lost or has trouble finding a parking spot, s/he will enter the test feeling stressed. This is not a good way to begin these critically important exams.

3. Students should drive with their parents or alone to the test site. It is important to remain focused in the time leading to the exam.

4. Make sure that everything is ready the night before the exam: driver's license, test admissions form, calculator, extra batteries (AAA), pencils, snack/lunch, change for the vending machines, and gas in the car.

5. Rest the night before the exam—no cramming and no partying!

6. Eat a "normal" breakfast. Do not overdo or underdo this meal.

7. You may bring water to the test center.

FINAL WORDS OF WISDOM ON TEST-TAKING

Prepare Ahead: Do not listen to the knucklehead who regales everyone who will listen with stories of how he/she "aced" the exam with no review, after a late night of partying and with one arm tied behind his/her back. The ACT, SAT and the SAT Subject tests are not easy. They require several months of consistent studying and test practice.

Watch your Attitude: Whether you are a laid-back type B (or Z) personality or a high-strung type A personality, be careful of your attitude. If you roll with the punches, great, just make sure to study and become familiar with these tests so that you can do well AND open college doors. If you tend to stress out easily and worry about things, preparing for these tests will help you, too. Preparation will calm your nerves and put you in charge of the situation.

Listen to your parents: Even if it is just this once, listen to your parents. When they tell you to make sure to follow the tips above, to eat well or just to study, throw them a bone and listen. You get points for listening to us; we let you off the hook for other things when we get to win once in a while!

No Late Nights: Every year, several of my students will decide that they don't have to follow the normal rules and get a good night's sleep before the SAT or ACT exams. They think that they can easily handle the five to six hours of lock-down of these exams. And, every year, I get frantic calls from students who have earned poor scores after not getting enough sleep. Check out the Stupid Student Stories below!

No Sleepovers: Now, if I tell you that you can't stay up late the night before the exam, what do you think that I am going to say about sleepovers for goodness sake? Sleepovers are absolutely out of the question for two reasons: lack of sleep and late-night freak-outs about the destiny-determining exam the next morning.

Hometown: Again, every year, I have parents, who for some reason, decide to take a family trip on the fateful test weekend and to register their student in some out of town/state test center. If you can avoid taking the tests out of town, do it. The scores are always lower as the kids move out of their comfort zones.

Parental Blunders: Parents, do your very best to be home AND supportive the days/nights leading up to the SAT/ACT exams. Try not to raise significant issues that will cause strife as the exams approach. Students may seem not to care, but they are roiling inside.

Positive Thinking: I believe that it was Henry Ford who said, "Whether you think you can or you think you can't, you are right." Positive thinking (and studying) will help to support positive results. If you are scared or feeling negative, do something about it. Join a class or a study group; pick up a review pack. Take charge of your own destiny.

STUPID STUDENT STORIES

Although I like and respect my students, they do make for a good story sometimes. Over the years, I have had students and parents ignore almost all of the rules laid out in the previous pages and diligently emailed to SAT clients. Just to illustrate my point, I am going to tell you about a couple of students who made fatal SAT mistakes. All of the names have been changed, of course.

Several years ago, just after the new SAT was created, one of our local high schools decided to hold prom the night before the exam. Many parents called with a request for advice about how to handle the all-important junior prom and the SAT exam. My counsel was "either/or, but not both." Either take the SAT exam or go to prom, but don't try to do both because you will end up doing neither well. Of course, rules are made to be broken and Emily, a straight-A honors student had to go to prom and just had to have one final crack at the SAT. What happened? Emily had a great prom, stayed out late with the love-of-her-life, drifted into bed in the middle of the night...and bombed the SAT. I fielded the hysterical call three weeks later when the scores arrived. Emily and her parents panicked through the college admissions process as her SAT scores showed a several-hundred point drop between her May and June exams. Emily did get into quite a few wonderful colleges and is doing fine now. Her prom decision, though, did create a much more stressful senior year than necessary.

A year or two later, another student, a bit of a nervous Nelly who had had great success in SAT class with me, decided that she just HAD to spend the night with her best friend the night before the SAT. And, Nelly's parents took the opportunity to go away for the weekend. Nelly and her best friend spiraled themselves into hysterics, talking about how hard the SAT was and how important a good score was to their individual futures. Hours into the mess, both girls were crying. Nelly's best friend's mother tried to calm the situation. Nothing worked. Nelly scored lower than she ever had in class on her practice exams and gave up sure scholarships. As a result of her low SAT score, her college admissions were delayed and she suffered a lot of angst, as she was deferred for early decision and all through the spring.

The moral of the story? Rely on the voice of experience. Please.

Chapter 4

The Student Resume

· ·

LAUNCHING ON YOUR JOURNEY

Before heading off on the purpose, construction and development of your student resume, I want to take a moment to switch our focus from you, the student, to the admissions office. Essentially, your resume will be the center of your application process. Preparing your resume will require some soul-searching. Who are you? What do you represent? And what is most important to you? In this two-page document, you will introduce admissions officers to yourself, a student who may spend the next four years on their campuses.

Your resume will become the cornerstone of your application process. The resume will distill your values and achievements to two pages. These values and accomplishments will be mirrored in your recommendation letters. When you sit down to write your essay, it should add more detail and dimension to the representations in your resume.

- ◆ Explore the Student Resume, cornerstone of The College Coaching Program
- ◆ Read Colin, Grace and Ally's resumes and Julia's commentary
- ◆ Fill out the worksheets to start your own resume

Again, step back and think about the admissions officer. Think about the credibility that you will garner as your resume, application, recommendations and essays develop a picture of you at your best with your offerings. The organization and cohesion of these documents together will allow the admissions officer to really consider you as a person. Other students who do not weave together the components of their applications will remain stick figures on computer screens; you will leap off the page.

As you continue reading, watch our three sample students, Colin, Grace and Ally follow these steps. Colin's passion is medicine. He tells us in his resume. His recommendation letter glowingly praises his science skills, drive and determination. Finally, his essay shares his passion by bringing an operating room alive. Grace's passion is service and cancer eradication. Her resume tells of her commitment to the American Cancer Society and "The Sarah Project." All of the recommendations reinforce her passion and commitment. Finally, Grace's "Got Hope?" essay shares her compassion, drive and goals. Ally comes alive in her resume, as she develops from an average student to a committed athlete and community servant. In her essay, Ally shares a poignant story of her own community outreach.

PURPOSE

Your student resume will be your key to the application, interview and recommendation request process. The Professional Tutoring Student Resume is very personal and does not follow the common professional resume format for several reasons:

1. You are a student, presumably a young person.

2. You want to remind the colleges of your youth and potential.

3. You want the colleges to consider you as a whole person who will bring a diversity of experiences and ideas to their campuses.

4. You are much more than any grades and board scores can reflect.

5. You want to provide the colleges with information that will not be included in, the rather dry, application process.

Professional Tutoring students have found over the years, that a neat and well-organized student resume has opened college doors for them time after time. A good student resume will support a student through the entire application process including:

Thought-gathering: Writing your student resume will be your first concrete step in gathering your thoughts on the attributes that you will be offering colleges in your admissions applications. Because your resume will only be two pages, you will have to decide which strengths to list, which activities are most important and what goals you have for the future.

Applications: It is much easier to fill out your college applications, as well as honors, leadership and scholarship applications, when all of your accomplishments and activities are organized in one document. Since so many of the applications are completed online, it is easy to leave out information and hit the send button. It is hard, if not impossible, to amend the application once it is sent.

Recommendation Letters: You will enclose your student resume with your requests for recommendations (Chapter 6). Your student resume will give your recommender great information to include in the recommendation letter. The more information that the writer includes, the stronger the recommendation letter will be with in-depth and personal information. Thus, the colleges will give the letter more weight.

Interviews: Most private and some public colleges offer opportunities to interview either on-campus or in your local area. Your student resume is a great ice-breaker because it gives the interviewer information about your activities and interests. By listing your three top strengths, you have a chance to brag (modestly). A good student resume can also save an interview from dire boredom. Think about the poor college admissions dean who has to interview one unprepared student after another; s/he searches desperately for a thread of interest to follow as a shy, nervous, sometimes unwilling teenager sits in front of her/him. The two-page student resume will leave a hugely positive impression on the admissions officer.

Chance Meetings: An FBI agent once told me gruffly, "I don't believe in coincidences." As a college coach, I agree that there are no "chance meetings" because you will be fully captaining your college process. So what are chance meetings and how will you use them? A chance meeting will occur at a college fair when you visit your target schools' booths at a college open house or at a college visit in your high school. After introducing yourself to the admissions representative and striking up a conversation, you can offer your student resume. There is a good chance that the representative will review your resume in his/her quiet time. A well organized and presented resume will indicate that you are a serious candidate and have gone the extra distance to prepare. Your resume may very well be your ticket into an admissions dean's heart.

A VIEW FROM THE ADMISSIONS OFFICE

Colleges want to invite active, involved students to join their student bodies. Remember, that most four-year colleges are residential, meaning that the students not only attend class together; they live together. They eat together. They socialize together. They often live and work in close proximity with their professors. They interact with the local community and reflect the values and standards of the college or university which they attend and represent. College admissions deans are considering all of these subjective characteristics as they review applications. The smaller the college, the more important the subjective criteria become. Your student resume will remind the admissions officers of how important it is to build campus communities.

One of the reasons that the student resume works well is that very few students prepare one. Many students careen into the senior year of high school with little college admissions preparation. Sure, they may have taken great classes or garnered good community service, leadership and work experience, but they have not looked at a college application, had an interview or sometimes even taken an SAT or ACT exam. A strong student resume can set the tone for your application file. It can put you in the driver's seat of the college application process in the summer before senior year. You can grab the attention of admissions deans before their schedules heat up, fatigue starts to sink in and the rush of applications hits their desks. You can put yourself ahead of the many other students vying for an acceptance letter.

ADMISSIONS BUZZWORDS AND WHY THEY MATTER

Grades: College admissions deans rate grades as the most important factor in selecting students. Nothing will save you from terrible grades. If you have the good fortune to be reading this early in your high school career, study, study, study, and challenge yourself.

If you are further along in high school and have some lower grades on your transcript, think about remediating them. If you earned a D in an 8th or 9th grade class because you were lazy or immature, or both, consider repeating the class online or in summer school. You can even take a similar class at your local community college. This effort may not change your grade point average tremendously, but it will show growth, maturity, spunk and willingness to work hard.

If your grades increased steadily in high school as you matured, follow Colin's example in his student resume and show the improvement year by year. If you suffered through a significantly difficult experience such as a family death or major illness, and your grades fell, take a look at the student resume at the end of Chapter 8 (page 202) which outlines just such a situation.

Course Rigor: Closely linked to grades is the difficulty level of your classes. If you are earning A's or high B's in certain classes, take the honors, AP or IB class the following semester or year. College admissions deans carefully scrutinize high school transcripts and are not impressed with the straight-A student who chooses not to stretch into challenging classes.

Board Scores: Board scores include SAT and ACT exams. There are some schools that do not require board scores for admission. They are few and far between. Do not count on opting out of the SAT or ACT and attending a four-year college.

Leadership: Once the colleges have vetted an application in "The Numbers Game," they are ready to look beyond grades and scores. Leadership has actually become a major like marketing or biology at colleges across the country. Leadership majors participate in competitions across the United States.

So what is leadership exactly and what does it mean to your high school student resume? Colleges are looking for students who come on campus and make a difference, students with vision who will take the college in directions not considered previously. Students who have consistently worked hand-in-hand with adults, impress admissions officers. These students have stepped beyond their high schools into their communities.

So, how does a fourteen, fifteen, or sixteen year old demonstrate leadership or even gain some leadership experience? There are the obvious routes including scouting, student government, and the Junior Reserve Officer Training Corps. There are also many other opportunities in the community.

Let's start with an example. Say that you are interested in helping the homeless in your community. You serve at a soup kitchen at holidays, Thanksgiving, Christmas, Passover. You enjoy the work, but basically just show up when your parents are feeling the need for magnanimity. How do you grow this interest of yours into a leadership position? How about volunteering weekly or several times a month? When you see a problem or think of a way that the food service could be run more smoothly, talk to an involved adult. Offer to make a difference. As you become more integrally involved in the soup kitchen, the adults, volunteers, and paid staff will take notice. They will begin to need your help, rather than helping you to fill your community service hours or parents' need to serve the community periodically. Once you develop experience and credibility, ask to join the Volunteer Steering Committee. Offer to take on a major project, perhaps scheduling, food tracking and ordering or something else that will help the organization to run smoothly. In these next steps, you will be taking on the mantle of a leader; your skills will develop and your maturity will increase. Now, when you ask the Volunteer Coordinator or Soup Kitchen Director to write a letter of recommendation for you, s/he will have clear praise for your accomplishments. You will have made a difference and will have earned the respect of many.

Several years ago, one of our three students found herself in a similar position. Grace had set up "The Sarah Project" in ninth grade to honor her friend, Sarah, who died of liver cancer at the age of 14. As the years went on, Grace became involved with the American Cancer Society's Relay for Life and formed Team S.T.O.M.P. (Sarah's Team of Motivated Power) . In her junior year, she gathered fifteen friends and family members, raised $2000 and participated in the spring Relay. The Relay ignited her passion for cancer support and research. Senior year, Grace dropped several other activities, including her varsity sports and dedicated 20-30 hours each week to the Relay for Life. She organized activities at ten other local schools, including a major assembly for 1400 students with a cast of 50. She recruited a team of more than 100 students and led them to fundraise over $25,000. Team STOMP, led by a high school and comprised of almost only teenagers, beat nine of the 11 corporate sponsors in fundraising, including such giants as Starbucks, Saab Aircraft and Lockheed Martin, at one of the largest American Cancer Society events in the state.

Grace's passion is obvious to all who know her. The American Cancer Society took notice and asked her to head up its new National Youth Council. They want Grace and her core team to teach them how to reach high school students across the nation. Grace's experiences with "The Sarah Project" and the American Cancer Society helped her to develop into a self-possessed leader. This confidence and competence shines through to colleges. It comes across in the resume and in interviews. The passion resonates through her "Got Hope?" essay and through her daily actions.

Service: Service has become an overused word in high schools and colleges across the country. Some high schools require service hours for graduation. Almost all honors programs, and AP and IB diplomas require extensive community service. Unfortunately, the majority of students begrudgingly perform their community service requirement, looking for the easy way out. Colleges can tell the difference between those students with a passion for community service and those who are only going through the motions.

Many students look to church/synagogue mission trips to fulfill their community service requirement. This is fine if the mission is your passion. Colleges are well aware that many students fulfill their passion for international travel under the guise of a mission trip.

Don't overlook service as a requirement of yesteryear. It is becoming more and more important. Colleges now call service, "civic engagement" and "social entrepreneurship". Some offer majors and minors in both specializations. As our political climate changes, I imagine that service will become even more critical in college admissions and even in the career search process.

Entrepreneurship: Since community service has become a bit clichéd, one of the new buzzwords is "entrepreneurship". A high school entrepreneur is a student who sets up his or her own small business and actually earns a "living" in his/her enterprise. Some simple examples include businesses such as dog-walking, babysitting or lawn services. Other students develop tutoring businesses or websites.

Work Experience: Colleges understand that some students have to work to support their families, to pay for college or to have spending money. They understand that a 20 to 30 hours per week schedule does not allow a student to participate in many extracurricular activities and often shortens a student resume. Still, you can turn your work experience into a great resume builder. Just as described in the leadership heading above, find ways to make your workplace more efficient or better run. Keep track of your ideas and how you implemented them. If you receive recognition, highlight it in your resume. Keep track of your raises and quantify the percentage increases.

The Angular Student: An "angular" student is one who finds a passion or two in high school and develops them. This student may have found his/her passion in the violin. In addition to playing in the school orchestra, s/he may offer lessons to elementary age students each week or volunteer with the local symphony. S/he may have combined his/her service hours in the local nursing home with leadership skills to develop a music program in the facility.

One of our three students, Colin, illustrates this point really well. Right before junior year, Colin found his passion in medicine during a summer program. Colin's passion led him to volunteer in the local hospital and to take emergency medical training to work with a rescue squad. Colin's resume shows his growth. Colin does not just say that he is interested in medicine; he demonstrates his passion over and over.

An angular student is more desirable than a too "well-rounded" student. This means that it is preferable to get involved in fewer activities, follow them through your high school career and grow into leadership roles. The colleges want you to bring your individual areas of expertise to their campuses and grow with them.

The Well-Rounded Student: The buzzword of old was "well-rounded," meaning a student who had lots of experiences in different contexts. It is important to not flit from activity to activity just to fill your resume. Do what you love and love what you do.

CONSTRUCTION CAUTIONS

Descriptions: One theme that you will read over and over in this book is that of telling a story, in your resume, in your essays, and in your letters of recommendation. Integral to the resume is the strengths section on the first page. When you list a strength, add a quick vignette or story to illustrate your point. Saying that you are a hard-worker without any back up will not convince anyone. I am including excerpts from Colin's and Ally's resumes below. Read the adjectives that they each used to describe their strengths. Do you get a sense from their 100 word descriptions of who they are? Ally's description is first and Colin's is second.

Strong Leader: *"I was the captain of the Junior Varsity Lacrosse team at my school and was rewarded this year with selection as Captain of Varsity Lacrosse. I believe I was selected due to my eagerness and ability to help bring the best out in others, to keep everyone smiling, and to encourage everyone to keep trying and never give up. Off the playing field, I am a Sports Section Editor for the school's yearbook and a Staff-Writer for the school newspaper. I am comfortable with giving people directions. I am able to handle all kinds of questions, and I do not fluster easily."*

Ambitious: *"I am determined to reach my goal of becoming a surgeon. During my junior year, I set the goal of earning the very highest SAT Reasoning and Subject Exam scores that I could. In addition to attending a rigorous class, I studied an additional six hours each week. The hard work and determination paid off as my SAT Reasoning Exam scores increased 600 points from my baseline exam."*

Now, do you get a sense from Ally's and Colin's 100-word descriptions of who they are? Did you also pick up on their careful tooting of their own horns?

Ethics: In this internet age, almost everything in your resume can be verified. Do not make things up! Colleges understand that student resumes reflect a young person. They do not expect anyone at your age to have solved world hunger or to have a viable plan to fix the stock market. Sure, you can "brag" (carefully and modestly) about your accomplishments, but make sure to keep them real and honest.

At one of my college visits, I had the chance to sit down with Patricia Patten, Dean of Admissions at Christopher Newport University. We were talking about students who pad their resumes. She told me about a young woman who came to CNU to interview for the competitive Honors Program. In her application, the young lady claimed to be bilingual. Mrs. Patten is also fluent in Spanish. The Admissions Dean told the student that she would be thrilled to conduct the interview in Spanish, since it was their common second language. You know where this is going by now. The student was nowhere near bilingual. She choked in the interview and was forced to admit that she had exaggerated her abilities. Needless to say, she lost the opportunity for a top program and scholarship funding.

Originality: I just learned another lesson this week from one of my students who did this very thing: DO NOT copy anyone else's resume! Sure, you can use the format and even some of the ideas if they are similar to yours but DO NOT plagiarize.

Humility: There is a little song that goes "It's hard to be humble when you are perfect in every way!" Be careful on your resume, in your application, essays and interviews, to remember the basic tenet of humility. Colleges want to know of your achievements; they do not want to hear an arrogant teenager or overbearing parent brag. Talk with excitement and interest; your point will get across.

Privilege: Colleges will see applications from children of privilege as well as from children of need. If you come from good fortune, be careful of how you phrase your community service and other opportunities in your resume. Remember to stay humble and grounded at all times.

I have heard and read repeatedly that colleges are leery of the now-common church mission trip. It is becoming more and more common for students to travel several thousand miles at the cost of thousands of dollars to "serve" the poor and destitute for a week. These mission trips are wonderful experiences for young Americans and may even promote cultural understanding between two different "worlds." Stay off your high horse in describing the contributions that you made in a week or two in an impoverished village in Africa or Haiti. We all know that the villages would be better served by receiving even a fraction of the costs of shipping high school students across the world. Instead, focus on the relationships forged, the lessons learned, and the maturity gained.

Recently, one of my students last year was searching for a way to answer an essay topic about a person who had inspired her. She did not want to use the standard answer of parent or grandparent. Katie searched and searched, and finally brainstormed her way to a young Sudanese boy who had received soccer balls from Katie's own fundraising efforts. Katie wrote about the boy that she had never met who lived in abject poverty in the Sudan, who played soccer with his village mates with a rock or a tin can, if one could be found. Katie had learned of these soccer games from her father, a military officer who had traveled in Africa extensively. In her essay, Katie described her own organizational and leadership skills in running a campaign to raise money to send hundreds of soccer balls and pumps to Africa, all the time focusing on the unnamed young boy who kept his spirits up in his war-torn country, playing soccer like kids around the world. Katie says in her essay this young boy helps her to re-focus when the kids at school are showing off designer purses, the cost of which would feed the boy's family for a year. She says that she remembers him when students are caught up in Facebook or other drama. She says that the young boy has become her inspiration to study international relations in college and to maybe, just maybe, continue to make a difference in the world. What admissions officer would not respond to this young girl determined to change the world one soccer ball at a time?

Finally, if you have had the good fortune to travel for leisure and perhaps practice a second language, do not couch it in terms of community outreach. Call a spade a spade and recognize with humility that you have had fortunate opportunities to travel.

DEVELOPING YOUR STUDENT RESUME:

If you are a freshman or sophomore, you have plenty of time to develop your resume's substance. If you are a junior or senior and just getting started, it is not too late to find opportunities for involvement. Look for leadership, business, and volunteer activities in your school and community.

A worksheet is included at the end of this chapter to help you develop your student resume. I promise that you will find strengths and qualities that you did not even know you had.

REPRESENTING YOURSELF

If you have not already, make sure to set up a simple, professional email address for yourself, e.g., Colin.McFimian@gmail.com, Grace.Bennington@yahoo.com, Allison.Leigh@aol.com. This makes it much easier for the colleges to connect your file with your email address.

If you don't have an email account because you only use Instant Messaging or one of the social networking sites, make sure to set up an email account specifically for the purpose of your college applications.

FORMATTING YOUR STUDENT RESUME

The Professional Tutoring student resume format follows. Plan on revising the resume several times, both for editorial and substantive changes. Remember that your student resume will reflect on you and your commitment to the process. Errors will NOT help you. Here are some tips:

1. Keep your resume to two pages with an 11–12 point font.

2. Use active language.

3. Do not use slang or texting shortcuts.

4. Photographs are not necessary and are usually over the top.

5. Justify both margins.

6. Proofread and spell check repeatedly!

A STUDENT RESUME SUCCESS STORY

Grace Bennington had great success with her student resume across the spectrum of filling out applications, interviewing and visiting with college representatives. Since Grace was ahead in the application process and had been accepted to all five of her target schools by the beginning of September, she decided to research her schools by visiting college fairs and open houses.

In visiting one of the college open houses in Northern Virginia, Grace had the chance to meet her favorite university's president. After shaking the president's hand and thanking him for accepting her, Grace handed him her student resume. Lo and behold, the president reviewed Grace's resume and took the time to email her.

In the email exchange, the president complimented Grace on her activities, as laid out in her resume; he specifically commended her entrepreneurship and her fluency in Spanish. When Grace visited the campus for an overnight open house, she had the opportunity to meet with several admissions representatives and the president again. Because Grace had already developed a relationship with the admissions office and the president, she was in a great position. The admissions representatives welcomed Grace with open arms because they knew of her; the student resume had created a buzz. In the Leadership interview, the admissions dean complimented Grace on her resume again. Two days later, the president called Grace at home, invited her to join the Leadership Program (250 students out of the class of 1250 and an application pool of 9000), several weeks before the competitions were even scheduled to start. Grace also received a merit scholarship with the program. She accepted the invitation gladly and looked forward to completing her senior year of high school. In October of her senior year, Grace had locked into one of the most competitive college programs in her state. Remember, this was the student who had been encouraged to consider vocational rather than academic courses in high school!

FOLLOWING OUR STUDENTS: COLIN, GRACE AND ALLY

As discussed in the first chapter, we will follow the progress of three Professional Tutoring students, Colin McFimian, Grace Bennington and Ally Leigh. Their student resumes follow. Take a minute to compare the resumes; you will see that each of the students has different strengths and that their GPA's and SAT scores vary widely. Note how the students' strengths and personalities shine through their resumes. Do you see how much clearer Colin, Grace and Ally are than they would be if they were represented solely by a college application? These three very different resumes demonstrate how you can market yourself and your strengths even if you do not have a high GPA or perfect SAT/ACT scores. A strong student resume allows the colleges to see you as a growing youth, someone with potential and goals. The resume helps you to become a more interesting person than the dry college applications do.

Some points I want you to notice in each resume follow:

Colin: Colin's roots are more modest than either Ally's or Grace's. This comes across in the background section when he talks about his dad's years at a community college. Colin shows incredible grade improvement by separating his grade point average by year and he takes responsibility for lower grades in his freshman and sophomore years and shows his moment of lightening-rod change. As mentioned before, Colin also demonstrates his passion for medicine through extracurricular activities. Not only does Colin talk the talk, he walks the walk. By finishing up with goals, Colin leads the admissions officer to wanting to be part of his success.

Grace: In her resume, Grace very quickly provides a human dimension by discussing her two younger siblings and describing her four-year-old brother as the "family pride and joy." She takes a risk in identifying herself as a Christian, yet continues in that vein to describe her extensive service work. Grace proves her dedication and work ethic under the sports section demonstrating growth as well. Her entrepreneurship is evident, as is her deserved pride in teaching other kids. Finally, like Colin, she leads the admissions officer to her goals, finishing with the plan to join "Doctors without Borders."

Ally: Ally's resume has the challenge of explaining a mid-C grade point average. She very quickly fleshes the resume out to reflect her outgoing and positive personality. She shows her dedication through years of the same sports and her ability to lead over and over. In her service activities, Ally demonstrates a caring and giving heart. By naming the projects, she makes them come alive to the reader. Ally's goals are not as lofty as either Colin's or Grace's, yet they are still compelling. Her determination comes through in the sentence, *"I intend to graduate from college in four years and compete favorably for a well-paying job."*

Colin's, Grace's and Ally's resumes follow.

Colin McFimian
11111 Park Avenue
Annandale, Virginia 22924
571.555.6565

Background: I was born on September 3, 1989 and lived in New Jersey until I was three. Afterwards I moved to Springfield, Virginia where I have currently resided in the same house for 13 years now. My father was born in St. Louis, Missouri, and lived there until he was 23 years old. He attended McCluer High School and then Florrisant Community College. He graduated with an associate's degree in political science. In 1986, he arrived in New York City. and married my mother in 1987. My mother was originally from Korea and went to Seoul University where she earned a degree in Nursing.

GPA: 9th grade: 2.56
       10th grade: 3.14
       11th grade: 3.71

SAT Reasoning: May and June 2007: (Best Scores)

Exam Scores: Critical Reading: 710 (97th percentile)
          Math: 690 (94th percentile)
          Writing: 560 (Essay: 8)
          Total: 1960

Strengths:

Diligent: Although my first two years of high school can be written off as definitely mediocre, I learned several very good lessons in these years. The incredible opportunity to participate in the National Youth Leadership Forum on Medicine after sophomore year changed my direction. With my eyes set on a career in medicine, I began to study harder. My grades increased from B's and C's to almost all A's. I volunteered at Alexandria INOVA Hospital and enrolled in college classes to increase my medical knowledge.

Ambitious: I am determined to reach my goal of becoming a surgeon. During my junior year, I set the goal of earning the very highest SAT Reasoning and Subject Exam scores that I could. In addition to attending a rigorous class, I studied an additional six hours each week. The hard work and determination paid off as my SAT Reasoning Exam scores increased 600 points from my baseline exam.

Responsible: In addition to working hard in school, I participate in several extracurricular activities including Model United Nations,

National Science Honor Society, Alexandria INOVA Hospital Volunteer Corps, and my church youth group. I have chosen these activities carefully to make sure that I have enough time to participate actively. As a hospital volunteer, I learned that work is hard and that the road to becoming a surgeon will involve a lot of dues (grunt work). The Model U.N. taught me about other cultures and international policy. The youth group helped me to grow spiritually and to develop compassion; it also taught me about the importance of servant-leadership and serving our communities.

Academics: Throughout high school, my favorite classes have always been science. Chemistry fascinates me. As of junior year, I have completed Biology, Chemistry and Physics. In Senior year, I will continue with my focus on science with IB Chemistry Higher Level and IB Physics. I have participated in the Annandale High School Science Fair every year and have won first and second places and earned a spot in the County Public Schools Regional Competition twice. As a member of the National Science Honor Society, I have helped to organize and run the Annandale High School Science Fair. In addition to these high school projects, I have also attended several academic summer programs, including The National Youth Leadership Forum on Medicine (NYLF) during my sophomore and junior years. In addition, I was chosen to participate in Lead America's Program on Medicine at Georgetown University.

Service Activities: To complement my honor society requirements, I tutor middle school students who are having trouble in school. I try to share my story of having to learn the importance of school. I also have volunteered at Alexandria Hospital since my sophomore year. I am looking forward to working in the Emergency Room department as soon as I turn 18 in September. In preparation for this opportunity, I am taking Emergency Medical Technician (EMT) courses at Northern New Jersey Community College.

Goals: At this point, my goal is to be accepted to a pre-medical college program. I intend to major in Chemistry and perhaps minor in Biology. After college, I will begin medical school on the road to becoming a doctor and eventually, a surgeon. I also wish to continue my community service work and internships in college. My greatest aspiration is to work overseas as a surgeon.

Grace Bennington
11658 High Street
Fairfax Station, VA 22039
703.555.9863
GraceBennington@cox.net

Background: On October 20, 1990, I was born at Arlington Hospital to David and Jennifer Bennington and have lived in Fairfax County ever since. My father grew up in Connecticut, but moved to Northern Virginia in 1987 to marry my mom. He works in advertising. My mom grew up in the north, as well, but since all of her family was from Virginia, she came to VA for college and never went back. My mom owns an architectural design firm and works from home. I have two younger siblings, Emily and David. Emily is in tenth grade this year at Jameson Secondary School with me. David is only four years old and is the family pride and joy. When I go to college, he will go to kindergarten!

GPA: 3.4

SAT Reasoning: May and June 2008: (Best Scores)

Exam Scores: Critical Reading: 590
Math: 540
Writing: 670 (Essay: 9)
Total: 1800

Strengths:

Scholar-Athlete: I have been an athlete since I was three years old and began swimming and ballet. Since then, I have participated in a lot of sports, including dance, gymnastics, tumbling, horseback riding, cheerleading and track. I strive to keep myself in good shape and to dedicate myself to my sports and to my team. At the same time, my grades are really important to me. I do my best to balance school demands with those of my athletics.

Dedication: I set high standards for myself. Once I set a goal, I work very hard to achieve it. In high school, I have narrowed my sports to cheer/tumbling and track, my extracurricular activities to service projects and working, and have dedicated every other minute to academics.

Compassion: I am a strong Christian and lead my life according to Christian values. I really like to work with people, especially those in need. My charitable efforts occur both at home with our foster kids and exchange students and outside with homeless outreach programs, Girl Scouts and the "Sarah Project" for cancer relief which I founded in eighth grade.

Academics: Throughout my high school career, my two favorite classes have been math and science, especially algebra. I entered projects into the county-wide science fair both my freshman and sophomore years of high school. During my freshman year, my team's project won third place. Last year, we earned an honorable mention. In addition, I am continuing with my languages. After ten years of Spanish in school, I enrolled in IB Spanish I (Honors Spanish IV), this fall and earned a place in the Spanish Honor Society. Senior year, I will take IB Spanish II. Right now, I am studying abroad at the University of Granada in southern Spain; it is amazing! I hope to study abroad again during my junior year of college.

Sports:

9th-11th grades:	Power Tumbling
10th grade:	VA Power Tumbling Champion-Level 5/6
9th grade:	Jameson SS Freshman Cheerleader
10th grade:	Jameson SS Junior Varsity Cheerleader
11th grade:	Jameson SS Varsity Cheerleader
9th–10th grades:	MVYC Summer Swim Team
10th grade:	SRCA Summer Dive Team
9th grade:	Jameson SS Junior Varsity Track Team
11th–12th grades:	Jameson SS Varsity Track & Cross Country teams

Service   My service activities include working with the Shepherd Center, one of Fairfax County's only day centers for homeless people, Operation Christmas, Girl Scouts (Gold Award candidate), Congressional Internship (Representative Philip Gingrey) and the four year "Sarah Project" for cancer relief which I founded in 2005. Junior year, I organized and was the Captain of S.T.O.M.P. (Sarah's Team of Motivated Power), Jameson's Relay for Life Team; our team earned donations of approximately $2000 for the American Cancer Society. S.T.O.M.P.'s goal for 2009 is 100 team members and $30,000.

Work History: In 2002 when I was in the sixth grade, I opened "Grace's Tutoring Service." My business began with an eighth grader who needed help in Spanish I. Last year, "Grace's Tutoring Service" blossomed. At this time, I have six students per week and specialize in Algebra and Spanish. My oldest clients include a junior at Auburn University (Spanish 101) and a sophomore at NVCC (Molecular

Biology 202) and my youngest is in eighth grade Honors Algebra I.

Goals: Right now, my goals are to succeed academically in my senior year. I am working to complete the Girl Scout Gold Award project; this requires a major time commitment. I love having my own business and want to further "Grace's Tutoring Service" through the academic year. In college, I plan to study psychology and pre-med. I like working with people and find the human mind fascinating. I intend to pursue a career in oncology. My ultimate goal is to work with Doctors without Borders.

Allison (Ally) Leigh
59875 Shadow Lane
Springfield, Virginia 22151
(777) 555-6490 allison.leigh@studentmail.edu

Background: I was born December 19, 1990, at the Air Force Academy hospital in Colorado Springs, Colorado, the second daughter of Jim and Alicia Leigh. My father attended The Virginia Military Institute. He also went on to earn several advanced degrees. My mother attended Central Missouri State University. I have two siblings: an older sister named Katherine who is in her second year at Christopher Newport University and a younger sister, Caroline, who is in the seventh grade.

GPA: 2.6

Scores: Date: May 2008
          Critical Reading: 460
          Math: 480
          Writing: 480
          Total: 1420

Strengths:

Determined: During my freshman and sophomore years I found myself struggling with school work. Recognizing the importance of bringing my grades up, I worked with my parents to obtain tutor assistance. I have been working with the same tutor for three years and with hard work, I have been able to significantly improve my grades.

Student Athlete: Playing nine years of club and travel team soccer and playing varsity lacrosse for Wheatfield High School has convinced me that good health and physical fitness is very important. I work hard to keep myself in good shape, and I make it a goal of mine to encourage others to find a sport they can enjoy.

Strong Leader: I was the captain of the Junior Varsity Lacrosse team at my school and was rewarded this year with selection as Captain of Varsity Lacrosse. I believe I was selected due to my eagerness and ability to help bring the best out in others, to keep everyone smiling and, and to encourage everyone to keep trying and never give up. Off the playing field, I am a Sports Section Editor for the school's yearbook and a Staff-Writer for the school newspaper. I am comfortable with giving people directions. I am able to handle all kinds of questions, and I do not fluster easily.

Academics: During my high school years I studied the French language for three years, and completed a year in American Sign Language. I have been a Staff-Writer for three years for the "Olympian", our school yearbook. This year, I am the Senior Sports Editor. I am also a Staff-Writer/Photographer for the "Oracle", our school newspaper. I am currently taking an Advanced Placement course called AP Human Geography in which we study about people and cultures around the world.

Athletics:

Soccer Clubs:
Springfield Youth Club Rec. League (1999-2003)
Washington Area Girls Soccer (WAGS) SYC-Xplosion
DIV-Starting Center-mid (2004-2007)

High School Lacrosse:
Freshman: JV Starting Attack (2006)
Sophomore: JV Starting Attack, Lead Scorer (Captain) (2007)
Junior: Varsity Starting 3rd Man Defense (2008) (Letter)
Senior: Varsity Starting Defense (Captain) (2009)

Recruited Guest Player:
WAGS SYC Galaxy DII Center Mid
    (2006 scrimmage team, 2007 team)
WAGS SYC Xplosion Prince Wm. County Labor Day
    Tournament (2008)

Service Activities: I enjoy helping others in need. Since my freshman year of high school I have been in the Key Club; this requires all members to complete 30 hours of community service through projects. During my junior year I volunteered for an organization called Christie's Christmas where each volunteer is introduced to a less fortunate child and takes that child to Target for a shopping spree of clothes and school supplies. My junior and senior year I participated in WSHS Beautification Day. My sophomore year I was the manager of the JV basketball team and I was a leader in the Lacrosse Outreach Program where I taught a group of 11-year-olds the skills and drills that the sport requires.

Work History: In 2007 I was employed as a Vet-Tech for Hometown Veterinary Clinic. I learned organizational skills, how to be professional, and how to help cats and dogs in danger. I have also learned to accept the responsibility of caring for others through regular babysitting jobs for toddlers and small children.

Goals: My goals for the future are to finish high school with good grades. After high school, I plan to attend college and study business. I intend to graduate from college in four years and compete favorably for a well-paying job. In the next 15 years I see myself working in the advertising or marketing industries, and starting a family of my own.

DEVELOPING YOUR OWN STUDENT RESUME

In addition to filling their campuses with strong academic candidates, colleges want to create communities of students, essentially large families. As in any family, each member brings strengths. The colleges call these strengths diversity. Colleges are trying to build a campus of involved, active and lively students, students involved in all areas of campus life: strong academics, research, band and orchestra, athletics, student government, outreach, service, etc. As it will be for you, the academic match is fairly easy; test scores and grades determine that suitability. It is the qualitative criteria that can make or break acceptances.

So what do you have to bring to the college community besides your grades and SAT/ACT scores? In the following categories, think about what you have that is unique?

Your academic experience: What is/was your favorite class in high school? Why? Did you receive any honors or awards?

_____

_____

_____

_____

Your family and background: Do you have a special heritage, life experiences or family? Tell about your experience:

_____

_____

_____

_____

Athletics: Have you participated in sports? At what level? Have you held any leadership positions?

_____

_____

_____

_____

Music and Arts: Have you participated in music or the arts? At what level? Have you held any leadership positions?

_____

_____

_____

_____

Service Activities: Have you volunteered in high school with school or community organizations? Did you participate in Scouting? Did you earn an Eagle or Gold Award? Tell about these opportunities. What did you learn?

_____

_____

_____

_____

Leadership Positions: Have you had a chance to lead other students and/or adults? Think about your roles in school, in the community and at work. If you have led, quantify (spell out with statistics/numbers) your impact. Notice on Colin's resume how he specified his study time to earn a strong SAT score. He also relates under "Service Activities," his leadership by sharing his story of "having to learn the importance of school." Grace specifies her Team S.T.O.M.P. successes, *"Junior year, I organized and was the Captain of S.T.O.M.P. (Sarah's Team of Motivated Power), Jameson's Relay for Life Team; our* *team earned donations of approximately $2000 for the American Cancer Society.* S.T.O.M.P.'s goal for 2009 is 100 team members and $30,000. She also very specifically discusses her tutoring service. These details make the resume come alive. Take some time to brainstorm here. You have probably done more than you realize. Describe your leadership roles below.

_____

_____

_____

_____

Work History: Have you worked in high school during summers or the school year? How many hours per week? What kind of responsibilities did you have? What did you do with your earnings?

_____

_____

_____

_____

Goals: The colleges understand that your immediate goal is to make your way successfully through high school and the college admissions process. Take some time to consider your goals for the next five to ten years.

_____

_____

_____

_____

_____

_____

Strengths: List three strengths and describe them, in just a few words, with specific examples:

1. _____

2. _____

3. _____

Now you have all the information necessary to develop your own student resume. Follow the format on the next page and feel free to refer back to Colin's, Grace's and Ally's resumes. Remember that your resume will grow with you. If you are starting this in the summer before senior year or even later, try to give yourself time to organize, strengthen and revise your resume.

Name
Street Address
City, State Zip Code
High School
Phone Number   Email Address

Background: Tell about your family, your background, where you have lived, basic information on your parents, your siblings, moves, etc.

GPA: GPA

Scores: Date:

    Critical Reading:

    Math:

    Writing:

    Total:

Strengths: List three strengths with strong adjectives and examples.

Academics: Discuss your favorite classes/academic pursuits.

Activities: Format your activities from 9th to 12th grades, both in and out of school. List any leadership positions

Sports: List your sports from 9th to 12th grades including positions played and leadership roles

Service: If you have been involved in service/charitable activities, list them here

Other Activities:

Work History: If you have held a job or jobs, list the position, dates worked and your duties.

Your Goals: Relate your goals to college.

NOTES

_____

_____

_____

_____

_____

_____

_____

_____

Chapter 5

The Application

The application is your entrance ticket into any college or university that you will consider attending. The application is the first real opportunity that the college admissions office will have to consider your credentials. As outlined below, there are many sections and requirements of these applications. It is important that you carefully complete the applications, making sure to include all of the required components. Over the years, I have seen very qualified students rejected from schools that we were certain were a shoe-in. A closer look always revealed a breakdown in the application process: a messy essay, typographical errors in the application itself, poor editing in the body of the short answer responses, late test scores, transcripts or other required submissions, etc. In your application, you want to show the colleges that you are completely serious about the opportunity and privilege of attending each individual school, that not only will you be an asset to the academic community, but also that you will be honored to attend, if admitted.

The college application process has changed significantly since your parents applied to college. Students are applying to more and more schools, often ten or even more. The applications and their plans have become more detailed. The process is explained below.

THE APPLICATION PLANS

Early Decision: The binding Early Decision application plan allows students to apply to college earlier than "regular" application deadlines, usually between November 1st and December 1st. Students may only apply Early Decision to one college or university. Under the Early Decision plan, students may apply to other colleges under regular decision, early action and rolling plans. If accepted in to Early Decision, a student must withdraw all other applications. In applying under this plan, a student commits to attend the college, if accepted, and to withdraw all other pending applications. In return for the early commitment, colleges will render a decision usually by mid-December. If a student is not accepted, some schools will enter his/her application into the "regular" admission pool. Others will deny the application outright. It is important to check the individual college's policies on Early Decision candidates.

In order to qualify under most college Early Decision plans, all exams (SAT Reasoning, SAT II Subject and ACT) must be completed by November 1st or 15th. These dates must be verified with the individual colleges/universities.

Early Action: The non-binding Early Action decision plan allows students to apply to college earlier than "regular" application deadlines, usually between November 1st and December 1st. Unlike under the Early Decision plan, under this plan, students may apply to more than one college. Upon acceptance, the student does not have to respond until the spring. If the college denies admission, the application may or may not be entered into the "regular" admission pool.

Rolling Admission: Under the Rolling Admissions plan, the colleges review and make decisions on the applications as the applications are received. Often the response time to applications is very short (under two weeks). It is wise to apply as soon as possible to any schools with the Rolling Admissions plan.

Regular Decision: Under Regular Decision plans, students apply to a number of universities with deadlines generally between January 1st and March 15th. Students are notified by April and must make a decision between May 1st and May 15th.

Accepting/Declining: Once you, the student, have received your college acceptances, you will have some important decisions to make. Remember to respond to all of the colleges who graciously accepted your application. It is an important courtesy. Make sure to follow the deadline decisions to respond to the colleges.

TYPES OF APPLICATIONS

University-Generated Application: This type of application will be most familiar to your parents. Most colleges and universities produce their own application and make it available by paper and online. Generally, university-generated applications are two to four pages long.

The Common Application: More and more colleges are beginning to accept the "Common Application." Much more generic than the University-Generated Applications, this application is accepted by hundreds of American colleges and universities in lieu of their individual application. The advantage to the universities is that it is standardized and may be easily compared. The advantage to the student is that s/he will not have to complete numerous applications. Some universities will request that an essay or short-answer question responses specific to their university be appended to the "Common Application." The universities which accept the Common Application say that they do not prefer their own application over the "Common Application." If you decide to use the Common Application, make sure to fill out the individual colleges' supplemental applications. These are available with the Common Application and will usually pop up when you input the colleges' names. AP and IB test scores should be included under "Academic Honors" in the Common Application. The Common Application is much longer and more detailed than the average university-generated application.

Paper Application: While paper applications are falling out of favor quickly, they do provide students with a good starting point or practice application for each university. Generally, paper applications are available from colleges on tours, visits, online or by U.S. mail. The advantage of this application for students is that it allows for proofreading more easily.

Online Application: Most colleges offer students the opportunity to apply online via their individual websites. The schools prefer this type of application because it ties into their admissions databases and sorts applicants electronically. The advantage of this application is that it allows for immediate sending. The disadvantage for many students is that it does not allow for correction once it is sent. Proofread online applications meticulously before hitting "send"!!

Application Fees: Generally application fees range between $25 and $75 each. Since colleges prefer the online applications, many are waiving application fees. In addition, colleges often offer free applications to students who apply in the summer before senior year. Students may apply for a fee waiver based on financial need.

COMPONENTS OF MOST APPLICATIONS

1. Application (paper or online)

2. Test Scores (order from CollegeBoard.org or ACT.org)

3. Family Information (may require parental input)

4. Short Answer Questions

5. Personal Essay

6. Teacher Evaluation (student resume very useful)

7. Guidance Counselor Evaluation/Report

8. High School Transcript

9. Letters of Recommendation

10. Agreement Page

11. In-State Tuition Verification

12. Application fee, payable by credit card, check or money order, generally

COMPLETING YOUR APPLICATION

If I can only convince you of one thing, it will be that neatness counts in the application as much as all of your qualifications, awards, GPA and test scores. I want you to follow a systematic and methodical process in completing your application!!

1. Do some basic research on every college to which you will apply. Begin by visiting the school's website. Spend an hour getting

to know the college. What does the school seem to prioritize, market the most clearly? Take notes. Do the college's values mesh with your own? Will you fit in and will you enjoy yourself and thrive? This information will help you in preparing your essay and in interviews. Plan a visit and interview, if possible.

2. Download the college's application and print a copy, even if you intend to apply online.

3. Make a folder for each college application. On the outside of the folder, list the required documents for the individual application, e.g., application, transcript, board scores, number of recommendations, essay subjects and number required, etc. Check each item off the list as it is completed and/or sent. Make sure to write down your user name and password for each college's website.

4. If you will be sending the application by U.S. mail, make a copy and save the original. Fill out the application, by hand, carefully. Use your student resume to jog your memory on activities. Highlight any information that you do not have readily, e.g. your parents' social security numbers, so that you remember to include it. Proofread your application carefully. Also, ask one of your parents to do the same.

5. Once you are ready, fill out the application on the computer or by hand, copying from your "practice application." Before hitting the send button or mailing it, proofread it carefully and make sure to have someone else read the "ready" copy. Nothing looks worse to an admissions officer than a sloppy application or essay.

6. Print out a hard copy of the final application and put it in the file.

7. Plan ahead to request transcripts, recommendations, etc. Plan on at least a month of lead time. Make sure that you have followed your school rules in requesting your transcripts, recommendations and that you have ordered board scores to be sent (SAT/ACT). Follow up to make sure that everything was sent and received by the admissions' offices.

CAUTION

I just cannot resist another reminder of the importance of accuracy and neatness in your applications. These days, computers do much of the initial work of sorting applications in college admissions offices. While computers are very useful, they do not have the brain power of a discriminating human mind. In short, they get confused by information that does not "fit."

To illustrate this point, let me tell you about one of my students, named Tim. Tim fell in love with Auburn University in Alabama. All sectors of the school seemed to meet his needs: size, location, climate, construction-management major, etc. Tim and his parents were excited to send the application off early in the fall. Unfortunately, Tim was not as careful in just one input in the application, his mother's social security number. The computer could not handle this one little mistake. The computer spit back the application repeatedly. Finally, Tim and his parents, Mom at home and Dad via satellite from his Army Command in Iraq(!) straightened out the glitch with the university. Although everything worked out in the end, the one little, very catchable error, held up Tim's application and financial aid package. Extra waiting time stresses out families. Many times, the wait can be avoided by being very careful to proofread and meet all of the application paperwork requirements.

WORKING WITH YOUR HIGH SCHOOL GUIDANCE OFFICE

Your high school guidance department will play an integral role in your college admissions process. It is important to get acquainted with your guidance counselor. Most applications will ask for a written report from your guidance counselor. In turn, your guidance office will probably have a form for the student and possibly your parents, to complete. These forms will give the guidance counselor more information about you. Again, take your time to fill out the form and do it neatly, with lots of thought! Request these forms by the end of your junior year.

A sloppy questionnaire will not motivate your guidance counselor to root for you in the application process! Remember, that actual examples will give the counselor and colleges a better sense of who you are, both in and out of school. As you will see in the sample questions below, you have an enormous opportunity to influence the recommendation. Attaching a cover letter and your student resume to the school forms will provide each more information and fodder for the counselor's recommendation.

As you read the sample questions, compare the questions to one of the sample student resumes. You will see how much the student resume will support you in the application process.

Sample Questions for Students:

1. What three words would you use to describe yourself? Why? (Give specific examples.)

2. Describe your academic strengths. (For example: organization, research, writing ability.) Give details demonstrating these strengths.

3. Describe your personal assets. (For example: tenacity, resourcefulness, reliability.) Give details that demonstrate these traits.

4. Describe accomplishments of which you are most proud (academic, extracurricular, personal).

5. Relate life experiences that have significantly impacted you. (For example: a personal obstacle that you have overcome, special circumstances that affected your academic performance, financial issues.)

6. What is your possible career, major, goals? Elaborate?

7. Which courses/teachers were most influential to you during high school? Why?

8. Describe obstacles and disappointments that you have faced in high school. What lessons did you learn and how did you overcome the difficulties?

Sample Questions for Parents:

1. Describe your child's outstanding personality traits.

2. Please explain any unusual circumstances, obstacles, or challenges that have affected your child's educational experiences or personal development?

3. What would you like a college admissions officer to know about your child? Please write a "brag note" about his/her strengths and achievements.

"SPECIAL" PAPERWORK REQUESTS

In addition to the guidance counselor's report, you will need to request other materials from your high school. Most schools will require three to four weeks of lead time for each request. Remember to plan enough time for the reports to be forwarded. Most schools have specific forms available in the guidance office, career or college center. If you have attended more than one high school, you may have to request your reports from each school separately. Check with your guidance office to see if this step is necessary. In general, you will need the following sent from your high school:

1. Transcripts

2. Secondary School Reports

3. Letters of Recommendation (counselor and teachers)

In addition, colleges will require that SAT and Advanced Placement exams be sent from the College Board. This may be ordered online from CollegeBoard.org. ACT scores must be requested from ACT.org

THE COMMON APPLICATION

In the mid-1970's, a group of 15 private colleges decided to work together to develop an application that could be uniformly used to apply to all of their schools. Over time, this organization has grown to include several hundred colleges and universities across the country. The advent of the Internet helped the membership of this consortium of colleges and universities to almost double. According to the Common

Application's website, **www.commonapp.org** 347 colleges and universities now accept the Common Application.

Why would anyone bother to fill out eight individual applications when s/he could just fill out the Common Application and be done? You may quickly change your mind about the supposed "simplicity" of this uniform application. It is much longer at 18 pages, not including the Individual College Supplement, than any other college application that I have ever seen. Most Professional Tutoring students choose university-generated applications.

THE INDIVIDUAL COLLEGE SUPPLEMENT

Some colleges will require applicants to download or otherwise obtain their own individual "supplements" to the Common Application. These supplements will be available on the "Admissions" sections of the individual college websites.

JULIA ROSS' ULTIMATE COLLEGE APPLICATION STRATEGY

Okay, so if you have been skimming this rather dry chapter on college applications, it is now time to pay extra, extra attention.

My goal in this book is to teach you to navigate through the college search and admissions process successfully and to your greatest benefit. Nothing makes me happier than to hear from my former college coaching students that they love their colleges and are so happy. I thrive on helping students and parents to find the right match without the terrible stress and fights that so many families suffer on the journey.

Recently, I received a note from a Professional Tutoring College Coaching graduate. It warmed my heart; I hope that it conveys the need to plan ahead and work methodically through the College Admissions Process. Here it is:

Dear Mrs. Ross:

I know a few years have passed but I thought you would appreciate an update. I graduated from Purdue earlier this spring with a 3.19 GPA, earning a Certificate of Superior Achievement in History. I can't thank you enough for pointing me at Purdue, there is no way I would have thought of it on my own It's pretty much become my home. The college coaching program really is a great idea.

I've also been accepted at Navy Officer Candidate School. It's a 12 week program, but once I've completed it, I'll be an Ensign in the U.S. Navy. Then I'll be going to Intelligence school to become a Navy Intelligence officer. Things are really looking up for me and I can't thank you enough for helping me get there along the way!

If you are feeling lost or just need a little help on the way, visit me at www.JuliaRossProfessionalTutoring.com.

So, here is the Julia Ross Ultimate College Application Strategy. This will work best for students who are reading this book before their senior year of high school.

1. Request the college admissions paperwork from your high school guidance office or career center by the end of junior year, if possible. Plan on spending several hours with your parents, giving detailed thought to questions and assignments.

2. Begin your research early. Focus on admissions deadlines, especially those schools that offer immediate or very short admissions decisions. Highlight the schools that offer the quick admissions decisions.

3. Rate your schools, safety, attainable and reach according to the guidelines in Chapter 3.

4. Visit all eight of your target schools, if possible. If it is not possible to visit all of the schools by the middle/end of the summer between junior and senior years, then focus on visiting your safety schools. Follow the guidelines in Chapter 8. As you visit these schools, imagine yourself attending them. Can you see yourself here? Do you think that you would thrive and learn here? Would you be proud to attend? Remember that you don't want to apply to ANY school that you would not willingly attend. Too many students make the mistake of pacifying a parent or guidance counselor by applying to so-called safety schools in which they have no interest, only to find out in the spring of their senior year that they have only been accepted to one or two schools, their dreaded safeties.

5. As soon as your safety schools, with the short admission decision policies post their applications, be prepared to complete and submit the application. Then you can sit back, often for just an hour or two when the admissions decision becomes available.

6. As your list narrows, turn your focus to your attainable and reach schools. It may be hard to believe at the very stressful beginning of the college search and admissions process, but this will get easier very quickly with an initial admission or two.

7. Plan visits at your attainable and reach schools (see Chapter 8 for specific strategies). Make sure to interview, if at all possible. If an interview is out of the question, bring your student resume anyway. Try to get a few minutes of one-on-one time with an admissions officer. At the very least, request the card for the admissions officer charged with your local area and high school.

8. Continue with your applications, email contact with the admissions' officers, school visits (tours, prospective student open houses, scholarship weekends, etc.).

9. Complete and submit your application as soon as possible in the fall. Again, consider the view from the admissions office. Earlier applications may receive more attention. Details may be lost in the winter and spring scramble.

This strategy may seem simple but it is critically important. All of the Professional Tutoring students have used this strategy with great success. It is hard to explain the major relief that this strategy will give you. Once you have an admission to a school that you like a good bit, you will be able to really focus on the several attainable and reach schools that are on your list. This will allow you to tailor your applications, essays, recommendations, visits and interviews to your favored schools. This direct approach of keying in on only a few schools works miracles compared with the scatter shot approach of applying to ten, 15 or more schools. The schools also notice students who consistently keep in contact, visit and submit timely, organized applications.

Finally, an admission to a "good" college will calm your entire senior year as your parents calm down. You see, we are all secretly afraid that our kids will not get into any college anywhere and will spend the rest of their lives living with us!

THE MONEY TREE

My kids truly believe that a money tree grows in our back yard. They are sure that this money tree reproduces prodigiously. I, of course, work hard to keep the kids away from the money tree, as they would strip every dollar.

One of the advantages of applying earlier to colleges, is the protection that it affords your money tree. Many colleges, particularly public schools which are trying to attract more applicants and private colleges offer free applications EARLY in the process.

One of our sample students, Grace Bennington, applied to only five colleges because her safety school offered her admission in early August. How many application fees did she pay? Just one. Her parents were grateful for the savings of $150.

Chapter 6

Letters of Recommendation

· ·

Many colleges request letters of recommendation from one or two teachers and a guidance counselor. Good recommendations, like good essays, tell a story. The best recommendations are tailored specifically to a student and his/her college of choice. When considering whom to ask to write your letters of recommendation, choose teachers who like and respect you. Many students have asked me about requesting recommendation letters from someone famous or politically powerful. It may surprise you that colleges would rather have a strong recommendation from the high school teacher who knows you well as both a student and a person than from your local Congressman or Senator who has never met you and is just doing a favor for a constituent.

Remember to keep your eye on the college admissions process. Step back and think about the reason that an exhausted admissions officer would take the time to read a recommendation letter about you. He/she is looking for more details about the "fit" between you and his/

IN THIS CHAPTER

- Learn how to choose your recommenders and how to effectively request strong letters of recommendation

- Read Colin and Grace's requests and letters of recommendation

- Develop your own ideas

her university. Letters of recommendation that tell a story, stick in admissions officers' minds. These letters have the potential to assure the colleges that in accepting your application for admission, they are making a good choice, both academically and socially. The colleges want to know that you will succeed in their school and that you will stay! In this vein, prepare to ask teachers who have taught you in the recent past. If you are in eleventh grade, you may ask tenth and eleventh grade teachers. If you are in twelfth grade, you make ask eleventh and twelfth grade teachers. Unless you are applying to a specialized program, such as arts, music, law enforcement, physical education, it is important to ask a core teacher (English, math, foreign language, etc.). Finally, ask teachers who genuinely like and care about you. Over the years, my students have found it best to request recommendations from two to three teachers by the end of their junior year. Even if students only need one recommendation, requesting two to three letters allows them to cover their bases in case a teacher moves, changes schools, runs out of time, etc.

As an educator, I have been asked to write many recommendations. Writing a good recommendation letter is not easy; it takes several hours and requires a lot of thought. With this mind, think ahead to what you can do to make the writing process easier for your teacher, guidance counselor or mentor.

First, it is best to make the request in person. Make an appointment to speak with your potential recommender. Prepare ahead of time with a request letter and student resume to give to the recommender in this initial meeting. The purpose of the letter and student resume is to provide background information to the teacher/guidance counselor/ mentor. In your cover letter, you must respectfully request a recommendation and thank the person for writing it. Remind the recommender of his/her role in your life. If it is a teacher, tell him/her what year you took his/her class, why you enjoyed it and what you learned. Make sure also to include specific information about your goals and how the college will fit your needs and how you will fit the needs of the college. By providing the request letter and resume and taking the time to speak with the writer, you give the teacher/guidance counselor/mentor lots of information to share with the college and the fodder necessary to weave a story. A good recommendation letter will reflect an in-depth knowledge of the student.

Please, please, please be aware that recommendation letters are time-intensive for the writer. Do everything that you can to facilitate this process including requesting recommendations by September 15 of your senior year. Request completion of the recommendation by a specific date: 3-4 weeks, at least, from the date of your request. Keep in mind that teachers/counselors/friends have a choice of granting your request. Also, specify whether you would like the recommendation letters sent directly to the colleges or returned to you to be included with your applications. Either way, make sure to include stamped and addressed envelopes (for each college). Remember, you want to make this process as easy as possible for the person who is taking the time to write a recommendation for you!!

Finally, keep in mind that the people who agree to write a recommendation for you are doing you a huge favor. Write a gracious thank-you note, by hand, as soon as you receive the recommendation letter. Later, follow up to let the writers know which schools have accepted you and where you will attend.

In this chapter, we will review recommendation requests from Colin and Grace and the letters prepared by their teachers and counselors. As you read the requests that Grace and Colin wrote to their teachers and mentors, note the details that they included. By reminding the recommenders of this information, Colin and Grace are setting the stage for the recommendations. The recommendation letters borrow liberally from the student resumes. By including the details, the recommenders demonstrate their personal knowledge of the students. As you read the teacher's and mentor's letters, you will see the obvious relationship between the students and the writers. These detailed recommendations carry a lot of weight in the admissions process. Take a moment to compare the letters of recommendations for these two students to their student resumes. Critiques will follow the recommendation requests and recommendation letters.

COLIN'S REQUEST, LETTER OF RECOMMENDATION

Colin McFimian
11111 Park Avenue
Annandale, Virginia 22924
703.555.6565

Mr. Timothy Johnson
Annandale High School
1156 High School Place
Annandale, Virginia

Dear Mr. Johnson:

Thank you for agreeing to write a college recommendation letter for me. The insight that you will provide about who I am and why I would be a good choice as a student will certainly help me in the application process. I appreciate the time-consuming nature of this process and your commitment to take your own time to help me. In order to facilitate your preparation, I have attached a student resume to this letter. This resume may jog your memory as well as fill in some of the blanks about my background, interests and achievements.

As you know, I have worked with you for two years in our incredible Chemistry and IB Chemistry HL classes. These are not only classes in which I have learned about cellular structure, fusion and grant development, but also I experienced first-hand the elation of watching cells combine exponentially.

During this year's science fair preparation, I learned how cells work together to duplicate DNA in our Group 4 Project. The time that we spent the whole evening in the George Washington University's lab waiting for the cells to split, I came to understand the hours and hours of hard work that researchers put into their projects. When you explained to me that many scientists spend ten years or more on a single project, I understood the dedication that is required. Before this year, I knew that chemistry and biology fascinated me and that I wanted to pursue a career in the sciences. This year, under your leadership, I learned that this dream is attainable.

Thank you, again, for taking the time to write my recommendation. It would help me to meet the application deadlines to receive your completed letter by October 19. I have included a stamped and addressed envelope so that you can return the recommendation to me. I will forward your letter with my applications.

Sincerely,

Colin McFimian

Enclosure

Critique of Colin's Request Letter

Humility: Colin begins his letter humbly requesting the teacher's assistance and acknowledges the effort required to write strong letters of recommendation. *"I appreciate the time-consuming nature of this process and your commitment to take your own time to help me."*

Reminder: Colin reminds the teacher of their relationship. He tells Mr. Johnson that he has taken two years of science classes with him. In providing the teacher with this detail, Colin sets the teacher up to provide more credibility in writing the letter of recommendation effectively saying *"we have worked together longer than the norm in a big city high school."*

Experience: Colin leads into the main point of the recommendation by reminding the teacher of the lead role that he played in the prestigious Group 4 project at George Washington University

Decorum: Colin finishes the letter with hat in hand, thanking Mr. Johnson for his time and effort.

The letter of recommendation Colin received from his high-school chemistry teacher follows:

Mr. Timothy Johnson
Annandale High School
1156 High School Place
Annandale, Virginia 22924

Washington University Office of Undergraduate Admissions
One Brookings Drive
PO Box 3403
St. Louis, MO 63143-0403

To Whom It May Concern:

I have had the pleasure of having Colin McFimian as a student in my IB Chemistry Higher Level (HL) class this year at Annandale High School. Colin is bright, motivated and hardworking. He has been both an example and a leader to other students in and out of my class.

While fulfilling other advance courses at the Annandale High School, Colin still maintains an excellent work ethic and grade in my college-level chemistry class, IB Chemistry–HL. The International Baccalaureate program is known for its rigorous requirement. The IB sciences, in particular, are difficult and require exceptional dedication from the students to learn the material and to participate in the labs and student projects. Colin has demonstrated exceptional drive, determination and ability in comprehending and learning the difficult concepts presented in this class. Colin has earned a position as one of the top students in the class.

In addition to his academic prowess, Colin consistently shows an aptitude for leadership. The IB program stipulates significant group projects. As a participant, Colin unhesitatingly takes on the responsibilities to ensure the group is focused on producing high quality work. Colin especially demonstrated his knack for leadership in the recently completed Group Four Project. It is a science department-wide project that involves extensive collaborations among the students in different fields of science. Colin organized group meetings and assured constant communications among his group members. He lent a helping hand to other students whether they were in the same group or not. As a result, his Group Four Project earned an A.

In addition to his academic excellence at Annandale High School, Colin is also an active member in the community. He volunteers weekly at the INOVA Alexandria Hospital and is also an active member of the Model U.N. Club.

I recommend Colin to Washington University in St. Louis with absolute confidence. He will excel in his studies through his ambitious and dedicated nature and become an excellent addition to your academic and social communities.

Sincerely,
Annandale Chemistry Teacher

Critique of Mr. Johnson's Letter of Recommendation

Tone: Mr. Johnson's tone is positive and very complimentary. He uses words like "pleasure". He describes Colin as *"both an example and a leader to other students in and out of my class."*

Story-Telling: Mr. Johnson repeats the story of Colin's success with the prestigious Group 4 Project. College Admissions officers are well aware of George Washington University's elite programs.

Details: Mr. Johnson illustrates his strong relationship and understanding of Colin by mentioning outside projects, pulled directly from the resume.

Recommendation: Mr. Johnson recommends Colin without hesitation: *"I recommend Colin with absolute confidence."* Recommendations don't get any stronger than this.

GRACE'S REQUESTS, LETTERS OF RECOMMENDATION AND JULIA ROSS'S CRITIQUE

Grace Bennington
11658 High Street
Fairfax Station, VA 22039
703.555.9863

Mr. Carl Nicely
Jameson Secondary School
4786 Bigote Road
Fairfax, VA 22032

Dear Mr. Nicely:

The time has come for me to start thinking about my college applications. I believe that I have been preparing myself for this moment and I am ready to accept the different challenges in my life. Part of the college application process requires that I obtain letters of recommendation from teachers. You have been my teacher and my mentor for the past three years, and I have learned a lot, not just solely about math, but life too under your guidance. It would be a great honor for me to receive a letter of recommendation from you for my college applications when the time comes. I have included a student resume for your review; it will give you some more information on me, my academics, and extracurricular pursuits.

When I first met you three years ago in my Algebra I class, I never imagned that we would make such a strong connection. You have saved me several thousand times, and I cannot thank you enough. Our discussions throughout the years have shown me that you had so much to offer, beyond the classroom and mathematics. I have been truly intrigued by your dedication to your students and to others. My parents have always told us that we need to walk the walk more than to talk the talk. It has become clear to me that it is part of our directive to share our strengths and gifts with those less fortunate.

My family has hosted 23 exchange students and foster children (ages eight to the 20's) from six continents since I was three years old. It is hard to remember any extended period of time when we did not have another person stay with us for a few weeks or even a few years. Although I had no real say in the matter since I was so little, my family helped to organize a program to bring young victims of Chernobyl to the U.S. to detoxify their bodies from the radiation of the nuclear plant explosion. I remember not being able to speak the same language as the children who stayed with us. Yet, we could play together for hours. After several summers of hosting these fairly young children, we hosted several exchange students from Europe. That was fun; I got to practice my Spanish and it was fun to have a real live college student in the house; they seemed very grown up to me at the time. About six years ago, we made the decision, as a family, to open our home to foster children. We had to undergo a home study, in which we were each interviewed, to become a therapeutic foster family. A therapeutic foster family provides a safe environment for kids who have been severely abused by their parents or other caregivers. This experience has really taught me so much about sharing and giving to others. It has not always been easy living with disturbed kids. I think that it has helped me to grow and to realize how fortunate I am in so many ways. It has also given me a determination to give back to the community as a student and in the future, as an adult. I think that these experiences have helped me to grow and mature in ways that a lot of other kids do not have. This year, I am working on a Girls Scouts Gold Award project to help the Shepherd Center solicit donations of some of the everyday items that I take for granted, like shampoo, razors and deodorant, which homeless people view as a luxury. I admire that in your busy schedule, you make sure to not lose sight of those less fortunate or in need.

You taking the time to sit down and talk with me means a lot to me. I will never be able to repay you. I consider myself blessed to have enrolled in your class at the beginning of my high school career. From the beginning, I knew that I would learn a lot more than I ever thought that I would from you, and not solely about mathematics. I loved the fact that you talked about your faith and your beliefs and for all of your help with my research papers, projects, and other assignments. It seems that many people get caught up in shallow ideas, and are not able to ever steer away from them. I want to make sure that I do not do that. As you counseled, I try to make sure to brighten the day of other people and to not reflect the image of a spoiled snob.

Finally, you understand the juggling that it takes to achieve balance between life and a sport. My JSS Varsity Cheer Squad practiced 20-25 hours per week, after school and on Saturdays. On Friday nights, we cheered at the varsity football games. Now I practice six days a week with the track team, and we have long meets on Wednesday evenings and Saturdays. In addition, it is also really important to me to maintain my grades, preferably at a 3.5 or above and to be to continue the Sarah Project and S.T.O.M.P. as well as "Grace's Tutoring Service".

Thank you, so much, for considering writing a letter of recommendation for me. I look up to you so much. Someday, I hope to have just a little bit of the grace and kindness that you embody.

Sincerely,

Grace Bennington

Enclosure

P.S. I have included an envelope for your convenience, please place the letter of recommendation in the envelope. I have not yet decided which colleges I will apply to, but I will let you know. Thank you!

Critique of Grace's Request Letter

Since Grace has several letters of recommendation, the critiques will be separated for your ease of reading.

Relationship: Grace reinforces the close relationship that she has had with Mr. Nicely, her math teacher and mentor, for several years. She acknowledges his importance to her: *"You have been my teacher and my mentor for the past three years, and I have learned a lot, not just solely about math, but life too, under your guidance."*

Gratitude: Like Colin, Grace expresses her gratitude for Mr. Nicely's efforts in writing her recommendation: *"It would be a great honor for me to receive a letter of recommendation from you for my college applications when the time comes."*

History: Grace includes details about her life that are not in her resume, including her childhood shared with exchange students and foster children, *"My family has hosted 23 exchange students and foster children (ages eight to the 20's) from six continents since I was three years old. It is hard to remember any extended period of time when we did not* *have another person stay with us for a few weeks or even a few years."* This bolsters Grace's claim in her student resume that she is compassionate.

Decorum: As a seventeen-year old girl, Grace adds a bit more mushiness to her letter than Colin does to his. Nevertheless, her personality shines through her request in the following words, *"Thank you, so much, for considering writing a letter of recommendation for me. I look up to you so much. Someday, I hope to have just a little bit of the grace and kindness that you embody."*

James W. Jameson Secondary School
4786 Bigote Road
Fairfax, VA 22032

To: Admissions Office: Roanoke College
From: Carl O. Nicely, Jr., Teacher
Date: August 15
Subject: Recommendation for Grace Bennington

With both a son and daughter-in-law who are Roanoke College alumni ('95, '96) and having recommended to Grace and her parents to visit your school, I strongly recommend her as a student who would both do well at Roanoke and contribute to the student body of your school. In addition to having been Grace's Algebra I teacher, I have worked individually with her for over the last three years and also know her family.

Grace is an exceptional and unique young lady who, in addition to being a serious and hard working student, has two definite and contrasting sides to her personality. When you first meet Grace, you quickly see a smiling, polite, unassuming young lady who seems so shy that she blushes when receiving a compliment or asking for help. It is only when you have worked with her to learn something that is difficult, watched her put in extra hours to perfect a project or seen her practice with the cheerleading squad that you see the tenacity, dedication and hard work that make up her inner drive to succeed.

Grace is well aware of her strengths and weaknesses and has the inner strength and maturity to allow her to overcome her natural shyness to seek help and take advice. She is an unusual student in that she is always willing to attempt new ways to achieve success. Even when Grace does not understand something, she does as much as she can on her own and then unassumingly seeks assistance with prepared and very specific questions that eliminate wasted time. She is the kind of student and athlete that makes teaching and coaching rewarding.

At all times, Grace continues to be a polite, sensitive and caring individual who has made the most of her opportunities of travel and meeting people of different backgrounds. She currently is studying abroad in Granada, Spain. Fluent in Spanish, Grace is also working on French. She gets along well with peers, family and faculty and makes friends easily. Grace has been fortunate to have a supportive family and school, but what makes her special is that she has been wise enough to use the assets that have been available to her. This was demonstrated last year when she was concerned for her close friend, who was going through a family crisis. Concerned her friend might try to commit suicide, she risked a life-long friendship to seek help.

In addition to working hard to succeed in a competitive school and being a fit athlete doing both cheering and track, she is an active Girl Scout, does volunteer work, has had a Congressional internship, runs her own tutoring business, and is also active in her church. She does this while maintaining her grade point average and was accepted into the Spanish Honor Society.

As a dependable, hardworking, likeable and caring young woman, Grace is the type of person you would want your children to be associated with and will be an asset to any student body. If I can be of further assistance, I can be reached at school or at home at the following numbers.

Critique of the Teacher's Letter of Recommendation

Credibility: Mr. Nicely achieves immediate credibility by establishing that his son and daughter-in-law graduated from Roanoke College whom he is addressing in the recommendation. He is not just recommending Grace blindly; he understands Roanoke's value system and is averring the "match." Mr. Nicely also increases his credibility by indicating his long-term (for a high school teacher) relationship with Grace and her family, *"In addition to having been Grace's Algebra I teacher, I have worked individually with her for over the last three years and also know her family."*

Tone: Like Mr. Johnson did in Colin's letter, Mr. Nicely describes Grace in glowing terms, *"Grace is an exceptional and unique young lady who, in addition to being a serious and hard working student."*

Storytelling: Mr. Nicely tells a vivid story that would stop any adult's heart in his/her chest. There is a good chance that an admissions officer will remember this letter. *"This [good judgment] was demonstrated last year when she was concerned for her close friend, who was going through a family crisis. Concerned her friend might try to commit suicide, she risked a life-long friendship to seek help."*

Details: Mr. Nicely illustrates Grace's diligence by describing her activities. He also gets one more punch in for her success with the Spanish Honor Society. *"In addition to working hard to succeed in a competitive school and being a fit athlete doing both cheering and track, she is an active Girl Scout, does volunteer work, has had a Congressional internship, runs her own tutoring business, and is also active in her church. She does this while maintaining her grade point average and was accepted into the Spanish Honor Society."*

Recommendation: Mr. Nicely recommends Grace without hesitation. By offering his home phone number, he shows how far he is willing to go for this student. Teachers do not routinely share their home numbers.

James W. Jameson Secondary School
4786 Bigote Road
Fairfax, VA 22032

Dear Members of the Scholarship Selection Committee:

It gives me a great deal of pleasure to present Grace Bennington, a member of the Class of 2009 at James W. Jameson, Jr. Secondary School, for your consideration. Grace has asked me to make some comments regarding her strengths in support of her application for your scholarship program.

Grace has a 3.5 un-weighted grade point average (GPA) with a 4.1 for the first semester of this year and has worked extremely hard to earn the grades that she has received. In addition to her strong academic background, Grace is a varsity cheerleader and a member of the varsity track team, is active in Girl Scouts, has done an internship on Capitol Hill, runs her own tutoring business and is active in her church as a volunteer. Also, she studied abroad at the University of Granada in southern Spain last summer and is currently the Director of Spanish Outreach for holiday giving at a local charity. Grace founded the "Sarah Project" for cancer relief in 2005 and also founded Jameson's Relay for Life Team with over 100 members from 10 Fairfax County high schools. Grace recently put together an extremely meaningful pep rally to raise awareness of cancer as part of her responsibilities for the Relay for Life Team. She has set an extremely lofty goal of raising $30,000 for the American Cancer Society, and I have the utmost confidence that our Relay for Life Team will meet this goal under Grace's tutelage.

The following excerpt is from Mrs. Alexandra Shepherd, one of our Middle School teachers.

"Grace Bennington was our private ray of sunshine in 2008. After our daughter, Cynthia, was diagnosed with cancer, she was able to attend school only two more days before her chemotherapy required her to be homebound. In each class, Cynthia's friends were sympathetic, empathetic and speechless as she told them the news. The outpouring of love and support was overwhelming. But as time goes on, everyone settles into a new routine and people become absorbed with the things in their own lives which need to be addressed. Grace's new routine included caring for Cynthia. I don't know how she did it, or really why... since Grace and our daughter only met in September in math class... but Grace's support was unending and unparalleled. Week after week she came to visit Cynthia carrying a bag of cheer...sometimes with other friends, often alone. From music and movies, pajamas and purses, food and flowers, cards and candy, scarves and even a smoothie maker...the wealth of gifts she collected from her own circle of support and delivered to Cynthia every week or two was more comforting than she could ever imagine. Each gift was a treat in and of itself, but the collective effort was a continual reminder that Cynthia was not forgotten in those weeks and months she remained home, isolated from her peers. Grace organized and orchestrated a show of support that helped carry our daughter through some very dark days. She is truly an incredible young woman and I can't imagine anyone more deserving of recognition."

Grace is an extremely effective communicator and she enjoys helping other people. In addition to the above-mentioned accolades, Grace has been involved in additional activities at Jameson and in the Northern Virginia community and has won many awards and honors.

I know that as a member of the selection committee, you have the difficult job of deciding which students will receive scholarships. I sincerely hope I have made your job easier by highlighting the accomplishments of Grace Bennington. In my twenty plus years as a professional educator, I can honestly say that Grace is truly one of the most sincere and hard-working students I have had the joy of knowing.

It is my distinct pleasure to present Grace Bennington for your consideration.

Sincerely,

Rick Beavin, Associate Principal

Critique of Assistant Principal's Letter of Recommendation

Credit: Grace's assistant principal begins by taking credit for presenting Grace's application to the scholarship to the committee, *"It gives me a great deal of pleasure to present Grace Bennington..."*

Accolades: Mr. Beavin lays out Grace's successes in the second paragraph by discussing her involvement in Girls Scouts, Congressional Internship, study abroad, her tutoring business, the Sarah Project and Relay for Life.

Furtherance: Mr. Beavin goes further by including an excerpt from another teacher. By doing this, he indicates that he has researched Grace's impact on the school community.

Story-Telling: Mrs. Shepherd's story of her own daughter's cancer battle brings depth to the recommendation. Mrs. Shepherd's testimony still brings tears to my eyes, a wizened old college coach that I am. She says, *"Grace Bennington was our private ray of sunshine in 2008. Grace organized and orchestrated a show of support that helped carry our daughter through some very dark days. She is truly an incredible young woman and I can't imagine anyone more deserving of recognition."*

Out-on-the Limb: Mr. Beavin climbs out on to a limb by saying that Grace is one of the most outstanding young people that he has taught, *"In my twenty plus years as a professional educator, I can honestly say that Grace is truly one of the most sincere and hard-working students I have had the joy of knowing."*

Robin Lyndon
Lynchburg College
Admissions@Lynchburg.edu
Office of Enrollment Services
1501 Lakeside Drive
Lynchburg, VA 24501

Dear Sir or Madam:

It is a pleasure to recommend Ms. Grace Bennington for admission to Lynchburg College. I have known Grace since she was three years old and as I have watched her grow into a mature young woman, I have been very impressed.

"Compassion-in-action" is the credo of the Bennington family. Arguably the Bennington family is successful on many levels – professionally and personally, yet they constantly seek opportunities to serve those less fortunate which is how they measure their own worth. As one of the founding members of the Christ Church Children of Chernobyl Program, the Bennington family hosted several Belarusian children whom were contaminated by the fallout from the Chernobyl nuclear explosion.

But that was not enough. They also opened their home to troubled teens and they have provided a loving and enriching sanctuary for many foster children. Grace recently told me that her family has hosted 23 young people from nine countries in her home over the past fourteen years. One young woman, a foster child, stayed for two and a half years and truly became a member of the Bennington family; Grace considers Cinthia her sister. Helping others is second nature for Grace.

Grace is quiet and calm by nature. She has very solid core values and follows her own moral compass with aplomb. Grace's modesty and quiet leadership is impressive and does not go unnoticed. Four years ago, after the death of a young classmate, Grace began the "Sarah Project" to honor her friend by raising awareness and funding for cancer research. Grace and her team of young people have touched the lives of other young cancer patients. The Sarah Project has included four local high schools, in addition to Jameson Secondary School. This year, Grace organized S.T.O.M.P., a Relay for Life Team of 25 students. The team raised $2,000 for the American Cancer Society.

Grace's wonderful, warm nature naturally draws people to her. Her small tutoring business helps both local paying students and homeless children. Grace has many skills that are well suited for this work – a fluency in conversational Spanish, experience in tutoring children who need academic help, a calm demeanor that comforts those around her, a kind and gentle deportment and a compassionate heart. In Fairfax County's very competitive educational environment, Grace maintains up to ten tutoring appointments per week, working with students in math and Spanish. Recently, she began to work with a 21-year old Auburn University student who needs help in Spanish. The fact that a 21-year old young man would agree to work with a high school student is certainly a testament to both Grace's command of the language and her ability to work with others.

During her sophomore year at Jameson as a Junior Varsity Cheerleader, Grace had the opportunity to meet the Captain of the Redskins Cheerleaders and the 2006 National Football League Cheerleader of the Year. Over time, she and Grace developed a strong relationship. The Captain was so impressed with Grace that she invited Grace to cheer at FedEx Field in Washington, D.C, at the sold-out Washington Redskins/ Atlanta Falcons game in December of 2006. Grace trained for eight hours with the Redskin Cheer squad and then performed at the half-time show in front of 98,000 people! This once in a lifetime opportunity demonstrates the respect that Grace garners from adults.

In the Girl Scout Gold Award, Grace has found the chance to develop her leadership skills and through the Congressional Aide program has learned how to improve the lives of not just dozens of people, but hundreds of dozens. As a retired Navy Captain, I have worked with many Eagle Scouts and Gold Award Girl Scouts and Grace will bring honor to this elite group of our country's youth. I am proud that Grace chose to become a Girl Scout at this time.

Grace's flame is burning brighter every year. After four years at Lynchburg, you will be warmed by the bonfire you have fanned in Grace Bennington. I recommend Grace without hesitation for admission and for significant merit-based scholarships. Grace is destined to make a difference in a troubled world. You will be as proud of her as I am when you see Grace in action. Don't miss this opportunity.

Sincerely,

Robin Lyndon
Captain, U.S. Navy, Retired

Critique of Community Member's Letter of Recommendation

Tone: Like the letters considered earlier, Captain Lyndon begins with the unconditional statement of recommendation. *"It is a pleasure to recommend Ms. Grace Bennington for admission to Lynchburg College."*

Credibility: Captain Lyndon sets up credibility in her letter by stating that she has known Grace all of her life, *"I have known Grace since she was three years old and as I have watched her grow into a mature young woman, I have been very impressed."*

Understanding: Captain Lyndon paints a similar picture to that of Mr. Nicely. She tells of Grace's quiet and shy nature, yet great success, *"Grace is quiet and calm by nature. She has very solid core values and follows her own moral compass with aplomb. Grace's modesty and quiet leadership is impressive and does not go unnoticed."* Captain Lyndon goes on to describe Grace's "Sarah Project" and her dedication.

Story-Telling: Captain Lyndon tells a lot of stories in her letter. Two that resonate with me, as a reader, is Grace's tutoring of a 21-year old male college student, someone four years older than she. Also, the story of Grace being invited to cheer at a sold-out NFL game paints an impressive picture.

Ownership: Captain Lyndon takes pride in Grace's accomplishment, *"I am proud that Grace chose to become a Girl Scout at this time."*

Recommendation: As befits a Navy Captain and executive, Captain Lyndon forcefully recommends her protégé, *"Grace is destined to make a difference in a troubled world. You will be as proud of her as I am when you see Grace in action. Don't miss this opportunity."*

Chapter 7

Application Essays

· ·

In the essays and short answer questions, you will have the opportunity to show the admissions staff "your personal side". Make sure that you write your own essay carefully and with a lot of thought. One of the biggest mistakes that students make is to submit a messy essay with grammatical, spelling and typographical errors. Messiness tells prospective universities that the applicant does not care and further, will not care in university classes.

Several years ago, one of my most qualified students, Daniela, decided to apply to the College of William and Mary, arguably the most selective school in Virginia. She had great qualifications: top grades and board scores plus significant extracurricular activities. Daniela wrote a beautiful essay about inspiration, loss and growth. Daniela used this essay several times, just changing the last line to include each university's name. The day that William and Mary's early decision application was due, Daniela did not have a lot of extra

IN THIS CHAPTER

- Learn why some essays are successful and why others bomb!

- Follow our three students through their essays and Julia's intuitive critiques

- Read the hilarious "Questionable Judgement" Essays

time; she had procrastinated. She made sure her application was all set and hit "send" on the computer. Six weeks later, Daniela got the bad news. She had been rejected by William and Mary when everyone including her teachers, guidance counselor and college coach had predicted her acceptance. Why? It was in the essay. Daniela's last line read, *"I look forward to four years at the University of Delaware."* William and Mary surely thought, "I bet you do." The moral? BE CAREFUL!

With perfectionism in mind, get ready to write a strong essay and short answer questions. Before beginning the paper or online application process, make sure to note each individual application's essay and short answer questions. Again, it is important to know the schools well. Spend time researching the college's individual website before beginning the essay. If possible, visit the college in person. Colleges need to know that you are truly interested in them.

In my experience, the best college essays have several characteristics in common. First, they answer the application essay prompt within the specified length. Secondly, great essays tell a story and draw the reader into that story from the very first sentence. This initial pull is called a "hook." As you read the essays in the following pages, notice the hooks. As you read, close your eyes after each hook. Do you remember the scene? After finishing the essay, consider what stands out to you: the story-line, the vocabulary, the active language, the poignancy, the emotion?

To whet your appetite, here are a few hooks:

The bright synthetic lights washed over me as I entered the operating room.

The bottle glistened in the corner. It caught my eye and with the irresistible curiosity of a sixth grader, I scampered over to see what it could possibly be.

Do you know that sick feeling you get in the pit of your stomach when you know something bad is about to happen?

Do you feel it? Do you see how these hooks set a scene and encourage further reading?

In telling a story, the student is allowing the admissions officers a glimpse into his/her life, values and priorities. Strong college admissions essays always draw the same conclusion: this student will be a good match for the university and will bring many good skills and experience to the university. This is also your chance to share your passion, whether it be medicine (Colin), leadership and civic engagement (Grace) or community service (Ally). As I mentioned at the beginning of Chapter 4 (Student Resume), this will be another chance to reinforce your values, beliefs, and goals for the admissions officers. Admissions officers have to keep hundreds of students' files straight in their minds; I can't even remember my three kids' names half of the time! By repeating your message, your story will become clearer and more memorable.

Next, remember that the admissions officers read hundreds or thousands of essays each admissions season, and that they are looking for freshness and an individual unique story in the essays. Try not to bore the daylights out of the poor readers! The final characteristic of a strong essay is that it is obviously written by a student. The student's personality and writing ability shines through, yet the essay is not so glossy that it appears to have been written by an adult or, worse, by a college coach! The college admissions officers want to get to know their students outside of scores and grades. Your essay is your perfect opportunity to morph from one dimension to three.

Over the years, I have compiled a list of do's and don'ts :

1. First and foremost, don't do anything stupid, e.g., writing your essay in crayon, changing the font every other word, paragraph,

writing backward, only in lowercase, or in a different language. Stop laughing; students do these things in the name of creativity!

2. Do not even think about writing about the six D's:

    - Depression
    - Drinking
    - Drugs
    - Divorce
    - Death
    - Dating

3. If you are going to write about difficulties, keep the initial description short and focus on the growth and the learning experience (see Chapter 8).

4. Keep your eye on the ball by remembering that the essay is your opportunity to tell the admissions dean about yourself. If, for some reason, you are writing about a historical figure or an event or someone famous, do not write a research paper. This does not help the admissions officer get to know you.

5. Control your hubris (in case, you did not memorize this word for your SAT/ACT exam, it means excessive pride). What I mean is, do not brag in your essay. Your strengths and skills will be evident in your student resume and application.

6. Keep your idealism in check: It is wonderful that you are young, full of enthusiasm and ideas but DO NOT TRY TO SOLVE WORLD HUNGER OR FIND WORLD PEACE in your essay. You will only appear silly. In consideration of tip #5 above, please do not suggest that your mission trip or any other activity has had a major impact on world hunger or peace.

7. Follow Directions: If the application asks for a 250/500/1000-word essay, check your word count and stay within ten percent.

8. Length: Generally, these essays should be no more than one page, single-spaced (two pages double-spaced) with a 12-point font.

9. Grammar Issues:
   - Do not use contractions
   - Use the active voice, as opposed to the passive voice
   - Use vocabulary words that you know. You will not impress the reader with words used incorrectly

10. Neatness counts and can make or break your essay. Right justify the essay's margins.

11. Begin your essay with a grabber or hook, a sentence that immediately draws the reader's attention.

12. Start your essays at least two weeks before you intend to submit your application. This will give you time to re-read the essays as the ideas form in your head. Each essay will need several revisions.

13. Ask your parents and English teacher to proofread your essay. A good proofreader would have saved Daniela from her fatal error.

SAMPLE ESSAY QUESTIONS

1. Evaluate a significant experience, achievement, risk you have taken, or ethical dilemma you have faced and its impact on you.

2. Discuss some issue of personal, local, national or international concern and its importance to you.

3. Indicate a person who has had a significant influence on you and describe the influence.

4. Explain how you would bring diversity to our college community.

5. Beyond your impressive academic credentials and extracurricular accomplishments, what makes you unique and colorful?

6. If you could have lunch with one person, living or dead, who would it be and what one question would you ask him or her? Why?

7. Discuss honor and its meaning to you.

8. Elaborate on one of your extracurricular activities.

9. Discuss an obstacle that you have faced and how you overcame it.

10. Who is your hero and why?

11. Why do you want to attend our college/university?

12. Write page 276 of your 350 page autobiography.

13. If you could change one aspect of your high school, what would it be and why?

14. Discuss your favorite author.

15. Write a personal narrative.

SAMPLE ESSAYS: THE GOOD

In the coming pages are eight sample essays, ranging from almost 1000 words to under 250 words. While these essays are included for many reasons including the strong writing styles and their great ability to tell a story, they were not all written by straight-A students headed off to Harvard and Yale. Several were written by students with a bare 2.0 average! How did the students do this? They wrote and re-wrote and re-wrote again.

As you read the essays, take note of the writers' hooks, active language and strong skills.   While you are at it, lose yourself in the stories. Readers always enjoy them.

As we are following our sample students through the college application process, Colin's, Grace's and Ally's essays are the first four that you will read.

Following each essay is a critique of the writing.

PROMPT: Describe a major life experience

The bright synthetic lights washed over me as I entered the operating room. Something about the sight was oddly beautiful: gleaming alien objects, polished to a silver finish, next to an immaculate table flanked by blue and white figures. Not long before, I never would have imagined that I could experience something as thrilling as a Whipple procedure at 8:00 a.m. on a hot Sunday in July!

This all started when I finished my PSAT and chose health as an interest, mainly because I was curious about that field. Soon after, I received a letter from the National Youth Leadership Forum on Medicine, a program I had never even considered. The program information was provocative: a dorm at Emory University for two weeks and educational and personal interaction with medical staff. The program would include shadowing doctors, observing surgeries in the Operating Rooms and attending seminars with all types of medical personnel including doctors, physicians' assistants and nurses.

Eight months later, a streak of blue flashed across the room as a laughing doctor flung scrubs at me. I saw my own fear reflected in the eyes of my peers as the doctor told us to turn back if we felt like passing out. What was I getting myself into? The doors opened in front of me; the lights propelled me into gear. Awe engulfed me as I watched the team of doctors and nurses surround a man who relied on them to save his life. Like a well-oiled machine, the team moved fluidly, gently invading the holy sanctum of the human body. I tried not to blink, determined not to miss a second. The surgeons first made incisions into the chest cavity then, with precise movements, started to cut their way to the pancreas in order to rid the patient of the malignant tumor on this vital organ. Adrenaline coursed through me, vaulting me to a surreal sense of high.

Hours into the surgery, the doctors started to shake their heads and pull out their exotic tools. I asked the anesthesiologist about what was going on. He looked at me with weary eyes and whispered, "This man has less than a month to live--the cancer has spread beyond his pancreas." A shiver ran up my spine. I turned to look at the patient's sleeping face, too peaceful for a body being ravaged.

Inside the locker room, my head spun. While collecting my thoughts, I heard the heavy footsteps of the anesthesiologist stop in front of me. In a grave voice, he told me something I will never forget:

"Doctors fight to save lives from death. While we do lose sometimes, it is still something special to watch the healed walk out of the hospital. There are very few jobs where someone can have such an impact on another and know that he is a part of that." His words stirred the new passion that the operation had lit inside of me.

Freshly determined, I strode outside of those doors with an abrupt, yet steadfast, resolution. While the sun shone upon my face, I looked up into the deep blue of the sky, my mind flashing back to that letter I had held one evening, less than a year before. I never could have guessed then how that piece of paper would change my life. Even though the doctors had not been able to save the man with pancreatic cancer, the experience left me with a sense of new life that has stayed with me since. I went back to school with determination and a purpose, to excel and surpass all of my peers. My grades improved dramatically from C's and B's to B+'s and A's. Since I now knew my purpose, I wanted to experience the hospital life more; I started volunteering at INOVA Alexandria Hospital. I love every minute in the hospital, the mundane and the fascinating ones. I know that the road to becoming a doctor is long and rocky, but I know just as surely that it is what I want to do, that one day I will welcome a wide-eyed student walking into my surgical room.

Word Count: 692 (Colin McFimian)

Critique of Colin's Essay

Commendation: Soon after Colin mailed this essay with his application to the University of Pittsburgh, he received both an acceptance and a letter of commendation stating that his essay was one of the most outstanding application essays that the University had received. He now attends the University of Pittsburgh with a major (60%) merit scholarship. How much do you think this outstanding essay helped?

Hook: I am sure that you did not miss Colin's hook, *"The bright synthetic lights washed over me as I entered the operating room..."* Colin's description creates the scene immediately.

Passion: Colin's resume and application talk of his plan to major in pre-med and to become a surgeon. His essay makes this dream come alive, *"Not long before, I never would have imagined that I could experience something as thrilling as a Whipple procedure at 8:00 a.m. on a hot Sunday in July!"* I almost have to chuckle as I read his excited words. I can imagine a whole lot of things more exciting than watching a Whipple procedure at 8:00 in the morning on a Sunday!

Credibility: Colin's words and excitement give his goals credibility. He really and truly likes medicine. We need passionate students who will become our nation's top doctors.

Humility: Colin recognizes his own limitations, *"I saw my own fear reflected in the eyes of my peers as the doctor told us to turn back if we felt like passing out. What was I getting myself into?"* Colin completely avoids the tempting error of making himself seem important to the surgery.

Growth: Colin eases in an explanation of his lackluster freshman and sophomore grades, *"I went back to school with determination and a purpose, to excel and surpass all of my peers. My grades improved dramatically from C's and B's to B+'s and A's."*

Goals & Dreams: Helping Colin to achieve his dream is alluring, *"one day I will welcome a wide-eyed student walking into my surgical room."*

PROMPT: Tell us about an obstacle and how you overcame it

The bottle glistened in the corner. It caught my eye and with

the irresistible curiosity of a sixth grader, I scampered over to see wh
it could possibly be. I-P-E-C-A-C syrup. "Hmmm, what is that doir
in the playground trash can?" The label indicated that it is used i.
cases of poisoning to induce vomiting. "Yuck! Who would vomit or
purpose?" As a third year safety patrol officer, I knew the appropriate
course of action. I retrieved the bottle from the garbage and marched
into the principal's office with my best friend, Preston. The righteous
indignation seethed from my pores. Preston and I felt great about
turning in a drug on school premises. We had been through all the
drug awareness training and were following the steps we had learned.
The principal thanked us profusely and sent us on our way...still who
would vomit on purpose?

As Preston and I sauntered into the hallway outside of Dr.
Rossini's office, we found out who would vomit on purpose; it was the
Queen Bee of the Eaglewood Elementary School and boy, could she
sting! The retaliation was swift and painful. Suddenly, Preston and I
were outcasts, ostracized by the entire sixth grade for foiling Raquel's
plot to become skinny and even bulimic. Pre-teen websites screamed
our names and identified us as the "narcs" of Eaglewood Elementary.
Raquel led by intimidation; students were either with her or against her
with no neutrality allowed. People whispered behind their hands and
no one spoke to us. Although Raquel and a couple of her cohorts were
suspended for several days for possession of drugs on school grounds
and improper use of the computer during school hours, the torment
continued in her absence.

The five months between that time and the sixth grade
graduation dragged on forever and ever. The kids snarled and made
faces at us. I felt bad for having made such a mess of the issue. In
my heart, I knew that I had done the right thing yet I still could not
convince myself that it was the smartest move that I had ever made.
The incident made a mark on Preston and me. Our friendship is

enduring even though we no longer attend the same school. Ironically, both Preston and I have risen to leadership roles in our schools and the community. Preston is the Student Government Association President at one of the largest secondary schools in the state, the same one that Raquel attends today and I lead several student organizations at Jameson as well as running my own business.

At Jameson Secondary School, I have found my niche as a student, as a leader and as an athlete. When I watch the girls on my cheer squad making fun of someone less popular or less perfect, in general, I remember how it felt to be out in the cold. I make a concerted effort to welcome new students to the school, especially those who do not speak English as a first language. Some of these kids have become my closest friends. While the incident will never leave my memory, I would not turn back time to change my actions six years ago; it taught me about peer pressure, about knowing right from wrong and about not losing sight of who I am and about leading with grace, strength and kindness. It has helped me, in high school, to avoid some of the social silliness, perhaps because I got it out of my system so long ago.

What went around certainly came around; several months ago, the retiring Eaglewood Guidance Counselor, invited me to come talk to this year's sixth grade graduating class. Of course, I accepted gladly. Preston joined me. I had to laugh at my sixth grade self, as I spoke to several classes of 12-year olds. They looked so small and harmless. How could Raquel have ever been so intimidating? We told them about the incident and about moving on. They stared starry eyed at me, the varsity cheerleader, and at Preston, the SGA president of 3,500 kids. I was honored. The opportunity reminded me that strength is borne out of adversity.

Word Count: 693 (Grace Bennington)

Critique of Grace's Essay

Hook: Did you catch Grace's hook, *"The bottle glistened in the corner...?"* This short sentence immediately draws curiosity. Everyone knows that some high schools kids drink alcohol. Could this writer be treading into that dangerous ground?

Transport: Grace transports the reader into the head of a rule-following sixth grader. She shares her own *"righteous indignation"*. *"As a third year safety patrol officer, I knew the appropriate course of action. I retrieved the bottle from the garbage and marched into the principal's office with my best friend..."* Can you imagine the scene? Grace takes a risk here in describing herself a bit negatively; how many people honestly want to admit to having been a bit of a dork?

Metaphor: Grace's metaphor about the "Queen Bee" is priceless, *"as Preston and I sauntered into the hallway outside of Dr. Ross' office, we found out who would vomit on purpose; it was the Queen Bee of the Eaglewood Elementary School and boy, could she sting! The retaliation was swift and painful."* Can you feel Grace's pain?

Introspection: Grace's essay is very introspective. She realizes that she did not handle the situation as well as she could have, *"I felt bad for having made such a mess of the issue. In my heart, I knew that I had done the right thing yet I still could not convince myself that it was the smartest move that I had ever made."*

Growth: College admissions officers want mature students and Grace's maturity is obvious, *"while the incident will never leave my memory, I would not turn back time to change my actions six years ago; it taught me about peer pressure, about knowing right from wrong and about not losing sight of who I am and about leading with grace, strength and kindness. It has helped me, in high school, to avoid some of the social silliness, perhaps because I got it out of my system so long ago."*

Personality: A good college essay will share the writer's personality. Do you feel like you know Grace? More importantly, would you want to share a dorm room with her?

PROMPT: Tell us about a time that you made a difference in your community (scholarship essay).

"Got Hope?"

These two words have become both a motto for me and a road map for my future. These two words are at the heart of the "The Sarah Project" and Team S.T.O.M.P. I founded the Sarah Project on December 20, 2005, my fifteenth birthday. Why would I choose my birthday to start a major project? Because the day before, I lost my dear friend, Sarah, to liver cancer. Perhaps Sarah and I had been naïve in the spring of 2005 when we promised each other that we would fight the cancer day-by-day. We looked forward to graduation, and swore that we would stand side-by-side together, victorious.

Despite all of the best efforts of Sarah's family, friends and the doctors, cancer, the determined killer, won the round. On December 19, 2005, cancer took Sarah, a daughter, a granddaughter, a niece, a sister, a friend and a Jameson Ram. And on that day, I made another promise to Sarah: to dedicate my life to fighting cancer. My fight began with "The Sarah Project."

Last year, I joined the American Cancer Society's Relay for Life, creating Team STOMP (Sarah's Team of Motivated Power). Fifteen students joined me in 2008 and the little team earned $2000. At the Relay's dedication ceremony, I again made a public vow; this time to come back stronger in 2009. In 2009, Team STOMP is the largest team in Northern Virginia and is still growing. Team STOMP has 125 members from ten high schools and a goal of $30,000. At this point, we are the largest team in Virginia and are ranked second in fundraising.

As I look forward from Jameson it is with bittersweet memories. In June, I hope to have the chance to address the Jameson Class of 2009 at graduation and the honor of accepting Sarah's diploma. We will be on the podium together; I promised.

Word Count: 312 (Grace Bennington)

Critique of Grace's Essay

Hook: This essay's hook lies in its title, "Got Hope?" Throughout the essay, Grace illustrates her hope.

Story: Grace shares the personal and heart-rending story of her friend, "Sarah." She shares a life-changing promise, *"Perhaps Sarah and I had been naïve in the spring of 2005 when we promised each other that we would fight the cancer day-by-day. We looked forward to graduation, and swore that we would stand side-by-side together, victorious."*

Compassion: In Grace's resume, she claims to be compassionate. This story personifies her compassion. When Grace describes Sarah, she recognizes all of Sarah's roles, *"on December 19, 2005, cancer took Sarah, a daughter, a granddaughter, a niece, a sister, a friend and a Jameson Ram."*

Passion: Like Colin, Grace says that she intends to become a doctor, specifically an oncologist. Also, like Colin, Grace describes her inspiration and in turn, determination. She promised.

Leadership: Grace applied for several scholarships based on community outreach and leadership. In this essay, Grace showcases her own talents with humility. She does not put her own successes ahead of the loss of a "dear friend". Rather, the dear friend is the inspiration for Grace's actions.

Theme: The theme of Grace's essay is a promise made by two girls. She repeats this theme three times, in the initial paragraph, *"We promised each other that we would fight the cancer day-by-day."* In the second paragraph, Grace makes another promise, *"and on that day, I made another promise to Sarah: to dedicate my life to fighting cancer."* The last sentence wraps up the essay dramatically with the fulfillment of the promise, *"In June, I hope to have the chance to address the Jameson Class of 2009 at graduation and the honor of accepting Sarah's diploma. We will be on the podium together; I promised."*

PROMPT: Personal Narrative

The best gifts I have received during the holidays of my high school years have not been wrapped in tacky tissue paper found under the tree or carelessly stuffed in my stockings. Kristi's Christmas was founded two decades ago in honor of a 19-year-old, former Wheatfield student, who died tragically in a car accident. During her life she frequently gave her time to help those less fortunate. Wheatfield High School students participate each year to keep Kristi's spirit alive. Each volunteer is paired up with a "buddy" and makes them feel welcome.

This year my friend Rachel and I chose two girls, Chandra and Ingrid, who were both 14 years old. We ate breakfast with them, made them laugh and shared our love. At first the girls were very shy because they were embarrassed of being less fortunate. Rachel and I made sure to show them we were not interested in their family's income or their living whereabouts; we were interested in what sports they liked, what music they listened to and who their boyfriends were. After we finished breakfast, we were to commute to the Target across the street. We dropped our buddies off as we were on our way out the door. We then met a small boy with glasses named Jacob. His caretaker explained that they were late and needed a buddy. Without hesitation I relieved her and told her we would be happy to have Jacob with us.

We had three buddies, $115.00 for each of them and only an hour and 15 minutes to shop. We rushed everywhere buying Transformer boxers, Hannah Montana P.J's, and every other article of clothing available within our price range. We went through check-out with just enough time and just enough cash. After shopping until we dropped, the kids were surprised as Santa Claus entered from the other room. Santa and Mrs. Claus read *"The Night Before Christmas"*. Then each child got to sit on Santa's lap and receive a sack full of goodies including school supplies, a sleeping bag and a teddy bear.

My most memorable experience throughout high school was seeing the children react to an outstretched hand, the offer of loving-kindness. The little kids leave happily with more gifts than they are used to. The volunteers and I leave happily without any material gifts. We get a new friend each year but the joy we take from it never changes. Too many people forget that the true spirit of Christmas is about giving, not receiving. Anyone who argues differently has not looked into the eyes of a ten year-old as she wipes away her tears and says, *"Thank you, this was the happiest day of my life and I will never forget it."*

Word Count: 462 (Allison Leigh)

Critique of Ally's Essay

Hook: Ally sets the scene right away in her essay for who cannot imagine a Christmas tree with gifts underneath it? Ally minimizes the importance of material gifts, instead pointing to the existential meaning of the holiday season, *"The best gifts I have received during the holidays of my high school years have not been wrapped in tacky tissue paper, found under the tree or carelessly stuffed in my stockings."*

Story: Like Colin and Grace, Ally tells an engrossing story. *"We had three buddies, $115.00 for each of them and only an hour and*

15 minutes to shop. We rushed everywhere buying Transformer boxers, Hannah Montana P.J's...We went through check-out with just enough time and just enough cash."

Compassion: Ally's compassionate personality shines right through the essay, *"at first the girls were very shy because they were embarrassed of being less fortunate."* Ally reassures the two young, insecure and embarrassed girls that she is interested in them, *"what sports they liked, what music they listen to and who their boyfriends were."*

Values: In sharing her compassion, Ally exhibits her values by quickly dismissing socioeconomic status as a concern, *"Rachel and I made sure to show them we were not interested in their family's income or their living whereabouts."*

Maturity: Ally shares her maturity. She says that her greatest memory from high school has been the opportunity to work with needy kids, not a concert, or prom or even a great teacher. In Ally's words, *"Too many people forget that the true spirit of Christmas is about giving, not receiving. Anyone who argues differently has not looked into the eyes of a ten year-old as she wipes away her tears and says, "Thank you, this was the happiest day of my life and I will never forget it."*

PROMPT: **Tell us about an important day in your life**

"Justin wake up, its eight o'clock!"

"Mom I don't want to go! Just let me sleep." Immediately, I bury my head with my pillow so hard that I can barely breathe. I crawl back into dreamland.

Fifteen minutes later. "Justin, GET UP!! It's 8:15 and you have got to be at school at 9:00."

This time all I say is, "Okay, Mom, I am going!" I get up and take my shower, put on my clothes and go downstairs to eat breakfast, lengthening each action, avoiding the inevitable. How does my mom come up with these stupid ideas? A growing experience, yeah, right! I pack my lunch and snacks, dreading the day ahead. "How long is this horrible day going to last? I hate the idea of going."

Now, it is 9:20 and I am late. I walk into the elementary school wondering how I got snookered into this situation. As I keep walking, all I see is little kids running all around me, at me. "Please kill me now! Already this is going to be a bad summer!"

Today is the first day of Rec-Pac and I am an unwilling "CIT", also known as a Counselor in Training. Rec-Pac is basically a day-care provider during the summers. It is fun for the kids but we older kids have to play all day with the elementary age children. When I had found out that my mother had signed me up, I was infuriated. Hanging out with little kids all day strikes me as a nightmare. I cannot imagine spending all day long with a bunch of snotty, little, leaking kids. We teenagers may be obnoxious but at least we have control of our bladders. All my free time in the summer wasted with little people!! What about my friends and my social life? I know better than to mention these concerns to the General, my mom. I can only imagine her response. Neither of my parents has ever believed in leisure time or the infamous "easy way out." Well now that you have the gist of this program, let's return to the fateful first day of Rec-Pac.

I walk in, join the big kids, the counselors, and introduce myself. "Hi! My name is Justin." They are all really nice and welcoming which definitely makes my sense of dread lift a bit. Looking around, I take in all the rug rats. As I watch a little longer, I see a little boy, maybe five or six years old, struggling to shoot a basketball into a full-sized hoop. As I watch, I see Charley's face line with determination. Yet the ball never reaches above the rim. At first, I look on, bemused, as he never makes a basket, yet continues to shoot, hurling the ball again and again at the hoop. Despite my best intentions to stay detached and to continue to resent this summer job, a little bubble of respect and admiration wells up inside of me. Finally, Charley heaves the ball with all of his might at the hoop. It sails straight up but ricochets off the metal with extreme force, whipping down to slam against his upturned face. As I watch in amazement and shock, I see Charley fall straight back, striking his little body against the pavement. This time, a new sensation boils in my chest. Is it fear? Finally, as if walking through a thick fog, I manage to reach Charley's side. I lean over to check the little body. How could I have let this happen to this little person? Amazingly, Charley stops crying, looks up at me and says, "Hey, I like you." "Wow, how do I respond to this?" Now, of course, I can never ever admit this to the General, but I have a purpose. I am influencing little lives.

Several weeks later, in the middle of July, I wake with no maternal prodding, grab breakfast and hurry out the door to arrive at Rec-Pac early. I want to see Charley, the little boy with whom I have forged a fast friendship. I look forward to spending time with him. He makes me feel so competent and mature, even taller than my six feet. When he falls or hurts himself, he always tells the other counselors, "I want Justin. Go get Justin!" Never a softy, I hate to admit how much this touches me.

The summer flies by and Rec-Pac is slowing as we prepare for the end of the program and the upcoming school year. Now, I do not dread going to my summer job; I dread leaving it. The last day of Rec-Pac dawns and I dread the ending all day long. And rightfully so, for it proves to be the saddest day of the whole summer. We, counselors stiffen our upper lips and say our goodbyes and turn to go. I stay apart from everyone else, watching Charley greet his mom. I watch as she takes his hand and they prepare to walk out the door for the last time this summer. All of a sudden, Charley tears away, runs to me and throws himself against my legs for one final hug. Muffled now, he says,

"Justin, don't go!" My heart tears and then I remember that I am the big kid here.

I kneel down to talk with Charley, man to man. "Charley, you have been a great friend to me this summer and I will miss you. I will be back next summer and will count the days until we can have a basketball challenge again." Charley looks up at me with soulful eyes and says, "Promise?" I do and I mean it. It has been a pleasure. I am ten feet tall. The General wins again.

Word Count: 959

Critique of Justin's Essay

Hook: Justin pulls the reader right in, *"Justin wake up, its eight o'clock."* Who has not been in this situation? Justin's reaction is comical, *"'Mom I don't want to go! Just let me sleep." Immediately, I bury my head with my pillow so hard that I can barely breathe. I crawl back into dreamland."*

Story: Like the other three writers, Justin regales us with an absorbing story. Justin outlines each step as he dreads the upcoming day. *"I get up and take my shower, put on my clothes and go downstairs to eat breakfast, lengthening each action, avoiding the inevitable. How does my mom come up with these stupid ideas?"*

Theme: Throughout his essay, Justin weaves in the theme of growth and his own size compared to that of the Rec-Pac campers. He does this so masterfully that you may not even notice. Each successive paragraph shows us Justin's transformation into a "big" person, a more caring adult. Examples include:

1. "How does my mom come up with these stupid ideas? A growing experience, yeah, right!"

2. "All my free time in the summer wasted with little people!!"

3. "Looking around, I take in all the rug rats."

4. "Now, of course, I can never ever admit this to the General, but I have a purpose. I am influencing little lives."

5. [Charley] "makes me feel so competent and mature, even taller than my six feet."

6. "I kneel down to talk with Charley, man to man."

7. "I am ten feet tall. The General wins again."

Comic Relief: Justin uses his sense of humor well, "we teenagers may be obnoxious but at least we have control of our bladders."

PROMPT: Personal Statement

I slipped them off for the last time, and unknowingly said my final goodbye. They had been through a rough day; one full of crowd surfing, mosh pits and incessant movement. I had put them through hell, yet they still managed to stay intact, shining brightly throughout the day. Delicate yet fierce, flashy yet subdued. My gold flats carried me through one of the best days of my life and were there through all the bad ones. Big things always seemed to happen when I wore them. Some good, such as receiving my driver's license, and some bad, like crashing my car exactly four months after receiving that license. Maybe it's because I wore them when I was feeling my most self-assured. Whether it was my mindset or the shoes, I always felt confident on the days I wore them.

My shoe collection was vast, colorful, and varied. Amongst the collection were patent stilettos, plaid Mary Janes and cheetah-print wedges. In a crowd like that, it's hard to be the "favorite." All were bold, and all made a statement, but one did it effortlessly, the gold flats. A sweet bow dressed up their tough visage, while the rounded toe and soft interior kept them comfortable. Their ability to match any outfit and add style to even the most basic look made them my favorite. They were my go-to choice in any situation.

It was a hot August morning when I was faced with a shoe dilemma. I opened my closet, and frantically searched for shoes to wear to an all-day music festival. As I peered into my closet, my gold flats seemed to be the glaringly obvious choice. They protected my feet, while allowing them to stay cool and lots of walking wouldn't be a problem because of their comfortable design. I hurriedly slipped them on and sprinted out the door, unaware that it would be the last time I would ever wear them.

I returned home that night and stepped out of my shoes, abandoning them in the middle of the living room as I ran to the fridge. Unaware of the tragedy that was occurring; I entered the living room with a Snickers bar in hand; unnaturally satisfied to be consuming thousands of calories. My contented mood quickly shifted to rage as I witnessed the disaster taking place. "Izzy, no!" I screamed as my dog viciously attacked my shoes, gold leather flying everywhere. I approached them slowly, for at first glance I knew they were destroyed. That night I threw my favorites in the trash, all five pieces of them.

Recently, I've tried to replace the shoes, but I've found nothing more than bad imitations and cheap designs. I've had to find new favorites now that my go-to shoes no longer exist. At basketball tryouts this year, I'll wear different shoes the day before, maybe even sneakers. I've realized that having the confidence to wear my gold flats is way more important than actually wearing them, and the self-assurance I once thought they provided, I've found in myself.

Word Count: 509

Critique of Hailey's Essay

Hook: *"I slipped them off for the last time, and unknowingly said my final goodbye."* Hailey piques the reader's interest right away. What is she slipping off? Is this essay going to take a turn for the worse?

Subject: Hailey chooses an ostensibly very light subject, shoes, gold flats in particular. Hailey's strong writing skills let her pull this essay off.

Passion: Hailey loves shoes, clothing and everything fashion. As a future fashion design major, her essay is appropriate to her passion. It shines through in her descriptions, *"My shoe collection was vast, colorful, and varied. Amongst the collection were patent stilettos, plaid Mary Janes, and cheetah-print wedges. In a crowd like that, it's hard to be the "favorite".*

Story-Telling: Hailey has a gift for story-telling. The reader can visualize her, a teenage girl, peering into her closet looking at all her shoes. The reader follows along as Hailey returns from a busy concert, heads into the kitchen for a calorie-laden Snickers bar and returns to find her magic shoes, like Samson's hair, torn to pieces.

Growth: Like all good college admissions essays, this one focuses on the learning experience of the applicant. Hailey has shared her passion and demonstrated her college-level writing ability. She finishes by recognizing that she does not need the shoes as talismen; she has unrealized strength in herself. She tells the college admissions officer that she is ready to move forward, *"At basketball tryouts this year, I'll wear different shoes the day before, maybe even sneakers."*

Adaptability: While Hailey waxes eloquently about her shoes, she avoids sickly sweetness or morbidity, *"oh, how, I will miss my favorite gold shoes."* Instead, she picks herself up from her loss, wipes off the proverbial dust and vows to move forward, *"I've had to find new favorites now that my go-to shoes no longer exist."*

PROMPT: Personal Narrative

Do you know that sick feeling you get in the pit of your stomach when you know something bad is about to happen? Yep, that is how I felt on the afternoon of June 20, 2007. I remember that day like it was yesterday. I had just returned home from seeing all my senior friends graduate at the George Mason University Patriot Center. Though it was a long and grueling morning, listening as name after name after name was called until all 600 graduates had had their chance in the spotlight, I enjoyed watching and daydreaming about my upcoming senior year at Lake Braddock Secondary School. I mused about how I would seize the moment on stage in the rite of passage from childhood to adulthood. With all the good happening, how could those butter-flies keep on fluttering in my stomach? Well, I would soon find out.

Upon arriving home my mom called out to me, "Maggie, your dad and I need to talk with you" and in those few short seconds my life, as I knew it, exploded: we were moving!

Now I have to be up front and honest and tell you that some time in my sophomore year I had begrudgingly given my blessing to my dad to start looking at different jobs in places other than Northern Virginia. As a child I had lived in Pakistan, Hawaii and India, and had traveled to Thailand, Scotland, England and France so the thought of moving was fun and exciting from a distance! Nowhere in my wildest dreams did I think we would move to Huntsville, Alabama and certainly not IN MY SENIOR YEAR!

The wildest dreams came true. After graduation, life sped up considerably. Instead of lounging at beach week, shopping, working at the barn, my family and I frantically cleaned, sorted and planned for the upcoming move. In a whirlwind, we stepped aside as the movers filled the massive truck in mid-July and took to the road. We arrived in Alabama at the end of July and before

I could even look around, school was starting. Who in their right mind starts school before Labor Day, much less at the beginning of August, in the sweltering heat of the Deep South? I will tell you who: The public school system of Huntsville, Alabama. I spent the first few weeks with my neck screwed around backwards looking toward Burke, Virginia, and all my friends at Lake Braddock. It was hard to walk forward with all my sights set on a school a thousand miles north. My mind was consumed with thoughts that I would never be able to live without my friends. Perhaps things would have been easier if my attitude had been filled with gratitude instead of reluctance. Nevertheless, I began the school year, in the middle of summer, and life moved on. I had not given much thought to what to expect once we arrived in Huntsville. Boy was I in for a shock at Senior Orientation!

Things were so different from Lake Braddock. I was a little scared at first, but I am glad to proclaim that I made it and a bit embarrassed to admit that I really, really like it here. Shhh, don't tell my friends in Burke; it might hurt their feelings that I am surviving and even, flourishing, here in the land of magnolias. And yes, I still have good days and bad days. But on the bad days I remind myself of the valuable lesson I have learned through all this......that I can depend on myself!

Word Count: 594

Critique of Maggie's Essay

Hook: Maggie's hook, *"Do you know that sick feeling you get in the pit of your stomach when you know something bad is about to happen?"* makes my stomach clench in empathetic response. Everybody knows this feeling and dreads it. Maggie makes the reader want to continue.

Tone: In this essay, Maggie's casual tone manages to overlay a sense of co-conspirator with the reader. While she is casual in her tone, Maggie is not inappropriately so. The casualness of the tone reflects Maggie's warmth, *"Yep, that is how I felt on the afternoon of June 20, 2007."* Maggie writes as if she is speaking with a confidante, *"Shhh, don't tell my friends in Burke; it might hurt their feelings that I am surviving and even, flourishing, here in the land of magnolias."* This sentence makes me feel like I am sharing a secret with a fun friend.

Personality: Maggie is well aware of her personality and she willingly lays herself out for the reader; one gets a sense of Maggie's high-spiritedness from her capital letters and exclamation points:

1. *"Maggie, your dad and I need to talk with you" and in those few short seconds my life, as I knew it, exploded...we were moving!"*

2. *"No where is my wildest dreams did I think we would move to Huntsville, Alabama and certainly not IN MY SENIOR YEAR!"*

Humility: Maggie admits to not having an open-mind to the move. She admits to being difficult and negative. *"I spent the first few weeks with my neck screwed around backwards looking toward Burke, Virginia, and all my friends at Lake Braddock. Perhaps things would have been easier if my attitude had been filled with gratitude instead of reluctance."*

Growth: By the end of the essay, Maggie's growth and adaptability are clear.

PROMPT: What work of art, music, science, mathematics or literature has surprised, unsettled or challenged you, and in what way?

Four years. That is one thousand four hundred and sixty days. In that amount of time a U.S. President can be elected and complete his term and a child can go from infancy to Kindergarten. It has been four years since I entered high school and now, in what seems like a lifetime later, I am finally graduating. Four years is a long time and yet that is how long it took Michelangelo to complete one of his most famous works.

The ceiling of the Sistine Chapel in the Vatican looks absolutely stunning in pictures, but I was privileged enough to see its true magnificence in person a few years ago. I was surprised to learn that Michelangelo had not exactly been enthusiastic about this job and because of the long periods of time he spent on high, uncomfortable scaffolding, he suffered extreme eye strain and neck and back injuries. Seeing the intricate and colorful depiction of human bodies and biblical stories at the top of this chapel impressed upon me just how much effort and sacrifice went into the project and how much focus and perseverance it required to see it to completion. Luckily for the rest of us, he never gave up despite the difficult circumstances he endured.

His work ethic and determination are an inspiration to me especially as I consider my upcoming college life and career opportunities. I hope that I will be even a fraction as steadfast and unremitting in the challenges that I will face ahead of me as Michelangelo was in his amazing work.

Word Count: 262

Critique of Kelly's Essay

Hook: Again, a gifted writer invites the reader into her story, *"Four years. That is one thousand four hundred and sixty days."*

Scene-Setting: Kelly helps the reader to grasp the length of time that four years really denotes, *"In that amount of time a U.S. President can be elected and complete his term and a child can go from infancy to Kindergarten."* Kelly immediately relates the time passage to Michelangelo's incredible work on the Sistine Chapel.

Privilege: Do you remember how we talked about privileged lifestyles in Chapter 4, under Student Resumes? I told you to be careful neither to brag nor to show false humility. In her essay, Kelly acknowledges that she had a great opportunity in visiting Italy; still she keeps the focus off of herself and on the great work that is the topic of her essay, the ceiling of the Sistine Chapel. *"The ceiling of the Sistine Chapel in the Vatican looks absolutely stunning in pictures, but I was privileged enough to see its true magnificence in person a few years ago."*

Inspiration: Kelly finishes her essay by specifically answering the prompt, "how did a great work affect you?" *"[Michelangelo's] work ethic and determination are an inspiration to me especially as I consider my upcoming college life and career opportunities. I hope that I will be even a fraction as steadfast and unremitting in the challenges that I will face ahead of me as Michelangelo was in his amazing work."* Kelly subtly compares her upcoming college years as a challenge, similar in their own right to that of Michelangelo.

SAMPLE ESSAYS: THE DAREDEVILS

Four "daredevil" essays follow. I have labeled them daredevils for various reasons, ranging from taking on a tough subject to discussing one's own faith. If you intend to take on a risky topic, do so carefully and with utmost caution. You do not want to send up the red flags in the admissions office. If your writings are dark, make sure to ask for honest feedback from your parents, teachers, and/or counselors before submitting them to any colleges. I hate to say this, but it is better to be safe than sorry, in the case of college admissions essays.

PROMPT: **What is the most pressing problem facing young people today?**

The most pressing problem facing young people today? It is three-fold: isolation, exclusion and apathy. As technology has increased exponentially over the past ten to fifteen years, essentially our lifetimes, community connections have disintegrated. Our generation, more than any previous generation, hides behind our computers, our cell phones, our iPods. We have lost touch with each other, with our humanity and the basic need to interact.

Recently, a horrifying documentary was released. <u>In The Bridge</u>, Eric Steel shows the result of 365 days of filming at the Golden Gate Bridge in San Francisco, California. The result? 23 out of 24 suicides caught on film. It is unthinkable; a film crew stood by and watched human being after human being, climb the massive guardrail of the Golden Gate Bridge and jump to his/her death. After a year of filming, the crew left to develop the documentary. In the name of research or psychology or art, this crew of human beings stood behind cameras, isolated from the intense pain of people ending their own life. The filming ended in 2004 and the documentary, hailed as "powerful," continues to sell on the internet. Would it not have been more powerful to intervene, to offer a hand, a smile, a connection?

Ten years earlier, a similarly powerful photograph earned a Pulitzer Prize. Kevin Carter, waited for two hours, in the oppressive heat of the Sudan, as an emaciated, collapsed child crawled toward a feeding center, less than a half mile away. Why did he wait? To observe a vulture who also waited patiently, just a few feet away. As Carter waited for the vulture to take action, the vulture waited for the child to die. After two hours of waiting, Carter had had enough. He packed his camera and gear and left. He left the child to die and to be eaten. Ironically, just three months later, the isolated, secluded and apathetic Carter committed suicide. I have to ask, would Carter have committed suicide if he had helped the starving child? Would he have been saved from the demons that would pounce on his soul had he had a purpose and had he intervened in such an incredibly powerful situation?

Our generation has never known a time without lightning fast communication and lightning fast opportunity. If we are to save ourselves, we must find a way to slow down, to reach out and to connect.

Word Count: 401 (Grace Bennington)

Critique of Grace's Essay

Hook: Grace almost does not have a hook in this essay. She delves hard and fast into a difficult subject area *"The most pressing problem facing young people today? It is three-fold: isolation, exclusion, and apathy."* In this hard-driving approach, there is no scene setting or invitation to join the author on a journey. It is stark and sterile, as befits the subject.

Risk: In this essay, Grace loses the sweet, natural tone that is evident in her first two essays, entitled, "Ipecac" and "Got Hope?." In this essay, Grace strives to convince a scholarship committee that she has a savvy understanding of her generation and that she can rise above her own age to analyze the weaknesses.

Evidence: Grace's essay is more analytical than the personal narratives or the creative essays. In this case, she uses data and hard facts to drive a point. At the same time, she infuses the essay with her own opinions: *"in The Bridge, Eric Steel shows the result of 365 days of filming at the Golden Gate Bridge in San Francisco, California. The result? 23 out of 24 suicides caught on film. It is unthinkable; a film crew stood by and watched human being after human being, climb the massive guardrail of the Golden Gate Bridge and jump to his/her death."*

Turn-the-Tables: Grace turns the tables on the reader by not allowing him/her to remain passive; she advances two rhetorical questions which demand a response:

1. "Would it not have been more powerful to intervene, to offer a hand, a smile, a connection?"

2. "I have to ask, would Carter have committed suicide if he had helped the starving child? Would he have been saved from the demons that would pounce on his soul had he had a purpose and had he intervened in such an incredibly powerful situation?"

Resolution: Grace avoids the trap of solving a problem so large as to be out of her realm. She diagnoses *"If we are to save ourselves, we must find a way to slow down, to reach out and to connect."*

PROMPT: Tell us about yourself in 250 words or fewer.

Church mission trip. High school student. Lonely old woman. Faith. Heaven. Tears. Life-changing experience. Me.

Barbara was a poor, lonely, disabled woman living in near poverty conditions in Appalachia. Her diabetes made it hard for her to walk and she was blind. Still, I could feel her love and warmth and wanted to get to know her. She told us stories about her estranged children, an adulterous husband who abused her, tried to kill her and then left her. As we were wondering how Barbara could radiate joy in the midst of such a terrible situation, she read our minds. Barbara told us that she almost died once, and that she had seen Heaven. She told us how beautiful, bright and peaceful it was. She began to cry, and said she wanted to go back. She said she knew it was where she wanted to be, and that she knew there was a loving God. Barbara told us that until she goes back to Heaven, she intends to enjoy life and appreciate all that she has.

I went on this trip wanting to make a difference in the lives of others. Ironically, it was I who was touched. This trip changed my life forever, and gave me an eternity of appreciation, love and faith.

Word Count: 213

Critique of Jessica's Essay

Hook: Jessica has the tough challenge of expressing her values and herself in under 250 words. To do this, she drops her hook with a staccato succession of words, *"Church mission trip. High school student. Lonely old woman. Faith. Heaven. Tears. Life-changing experience. Me."*

Risk: Jessica takes a couple of risks in this essay. First she breaks one of the cardinal rules of college admissions essays by writing about a church mission trip. Secondly, she takes the huge risk of declaring her faith.

Compassion: Jessica is one of the most compassionate people that I have ever known. If you have a feeling, Jessica will share it with you. If you ever need a shoulder to cry on, Jessica is the friend to seek. In this very short essay, Jessica shares her compassion and kindness. She relates to an old woman whom society has virtually thrown away. Unlike the stereotypical teenager, Jessica actually takes the time to learn from a poor, toothless old woman. The story tells us a lot about who Jessica is and her extraordinary values.

Humility: Jessica finishes the story humbly, saying that she had embarked on the mission trip with the typical goal of helping others. Instead, it was Jessica who was changed, *"I went on this trip wanting to make a difference in the lives of others. Ironically, it was I who was touched. This trip changed my life forever, and gave me an eternity of appreciation, love and faith."*

Sometimes, colleges will request a creative or analytical writing sample. The writer of the two essays below has a literary gift, inarguably. In sharing these two essays, she explained that they were both fictional, garnered from stories and experiences of friends. I think that they are well enough written to be shared, but are definitely straddling the line between risky and disturbing.

"The Rules I Learned in Kindergarten"

This is what I learned in kindergarten; the rules of life: don't hit, don't push and most importantly, keep your hands to yourself. Sounds simple, right? Well then how come this sixty-year-old man cannot seem to understand rule number three, "keep your hands to yourself'? "Leave me alone", pleads the young girl. "Please stop, please!" The man whispers in her ear, "You are helping me. Promise not to tell; it is our special secret, remember?" The child fights back tears, and says, "I won't. I promise." All the while, I wonder, what happened to the rules we learned in kindergarten?

Word Count: 100

"Greg"

Something is not right. Something is not right! Oh what could it be? Tears stream down my mother's face. "Greg has leukemia", she says quietly, "stage four." I feel nauseous, light-headed. My world has been turned upside down within seconds. I run up to Greg's room. He is sitting upright on his bed. I nearly knock him over, hugging him, "I love you", I say, "I love you too." Our lives have changed dramatically since then. That was a couple of years ago. Nowadays when something does not go the way it is supposed to, I remember my mother's powerful words, "Greg is alive".

Word Count: 106

SAMPLE ESSAYS: THOSE OF QUESTIONABLE JUDGMENT

I hope that you enjoyed the essays above, the good and the daredevils. I can report happily that all of the authors were accepted to college and all are contentedly enrolled at the college of their choice.

What differentiates a winning college essay from a loser outside of the do and don't tips provided at the beginning of this chapter? Strong essays tell a story; they use active and imaginative language and they do not bore the reader and they especially do not horrify the reader! Some examples of "questionable judgment" essays follow:

After I told my mom how I was feeling, we went to see my psychiatrist. I explained to him the situation and he came to the conclusion that my bipolar disorder was worsening. He prescribed a medication and said that I should talk to my psychologist again. Unfortunately, the medicine that the psychiatrist gave me mixed with my anti-seizure medicine and I developed a severe eating disorder.

What is wrong with this essay? It is way, way, way too personal. No one wants to know this much information. After the student decided to delete the essay completely, she laughed about the poor college admissions officer having to read about the depressed, epileptic, anorexic student who wanted to join the university!

In the beginning of my sophomore year, I became involved in a relationship that led me to emotions, obstacles and experiences I never would have thought possible. I was dating someone two years older than me and we unexpectedly became very serious. This was not some casual high school boyfriend; I ended up being with him for two years. We talked about the future, and thought we would continue the relationship throughout college. There were a few problems in our relationship which were not exactly minor problems. We strongly differed in our religious beliefs, which would make a future together very difficult, and nearly impossible. In addition, he had decided to join the Air Force, so he was already making plans to settle down and take the step into his adulthood. He wanted me to someday convert from my faith to his, get married, and possibly even go to college where he was stationed. I realized that his goals were very different than mine. I loved him and wanted to support him.

What is wrong with this essay? Again, the subject matter is too personal for a college essay. The colleges want to know how the applicants will succeed and add to the campus culture; this essay does not add any value to the application.

NOTES

_____

_____

_____

_____

_____

_____

_____

_____

_____

_____

Chapter 8

Giving and Receiving
An Impression

· ·

WHY VISIT?

With access to the Internet, why would anyone bother to visit a college before applying and receiving an acceptance? I have a lot of students and parents ask me this very same question. On one hand, it certainly seems like visiting five, ten or even fifteen colleges, just for the sake of visiting is very time consuming and costly. I agree that you don't want to run willy-nilly all over, visiting every college that you have ever considered. Nevertheless, college visits are integral to the college search and admissions process for quite a few reasons.

First, you cannot get a true impression without stepping foot on the campus and getting a feel for the school and its environs. Visiting colleges is like going on blind dates. Everything may look perfect on paper (in marketing brochures, posters, at college fairs, etc), yet when you meet in person, you know that this is absolutely the WORST fit

- Learn how to make the most of your college visits and how to open doors other students don't even know exist!

- "Romance the Admissions Officer"

that you can imagine. At the same time, a good match feels like "love at first sight". As your visit progresses, you will think of yourself in class, living in a dorm or attending sports events at this school.

Second, a college visit will answer questions that you did not even know that you had. Again, like a blind date, there is a limited number of questions and issues that you can consider ahead of time. As you visit, you will develop a sense of the school: its spirit, its values, its soul. Even though colleges use their admissions tours and open house events and information sessions to market their programs to prospective applicants (customers) you will be able to read between the lines and form an opinion. You will have your own impression, separate from that of your parents, your guidance counselor and your friends. Visiting will help you to decide if the college lives up to its brochures and marketing machine.

Third, remember to consider the view from the admissions office. College visits allow the colleges to see you and consider you as a person, rather than just another application. College visits give the colleges a chance to show off their offerings. The smaller the college, generally, the more interaction that you will have with the admissions office, professors, coaches, and possibly even the administration. During a college visit, you may have the chance to interview or participate in a small group student session. In this type of forum, the interviewer or group leader will form a, hopefully, favorable impression of you.

CAMPUS VISIT 101

Since the purpose of the college visit is to get to know the college, don't count on a drive-by visit or an otherwise quick run through. The minimum for any visit should include:

- The information session
- Guided tour
- Interview, if at all possible
- A meal in the college dining hall

This basic visit will take three to four hours.

SETTING UP YOUR CAMPUS VISITS

Many schools offer weekend as well as weekday visits, including tours and information sessions. The larger schools often have two sessions set up daily. Sometimes, the smaller schools are more flexible and can accommodate individual schedules.

Again, the Internet has changed much of the way that college admissions offices conduct business. Just a few years ago, students and parents set up tours by calling the colleges' individual admissions offices. Now, almost all college visits are set up online. In general, colleges have easy domain names (colorado.edu, uconn.edu, washington.edu, etc.) If you do not know the college domain names, most search engines will pull them right up. College websites always have a tab for the admissions office usually with a link to college tours and information sessions. You can register for both online. If an interview is not offered on the site, feel free to call or email the admissions office to request this invaluable opportunity.

The question of when is the best time to visit always arises with my students. It would seem fairly obvious, the best time to visit is on a weekday during the college academic year when students are on campus and in class. This is the best time to visit, to really observe the school in full swing. The hitch? It is just not always possible. By the time that you are reading this, it may be the summer before your senior year or even during your senior year when you cannot afford to miss school to visit colleges (or do anything else, for that matter).

As I mentioned earlier, many schools offer visiting opportunities on the weekends, on holidays and in the summer. When the college is not in session (or only in partial session, e.g., in the summer), you can still visit. Most admissions offices are open year-round and offer tours and information sessions. Just visiting a college, listening to an information session and getting to talk to a student tour guide will give you a perspective on the school. You will know if you like the school, if you think that you want to apply, and if you want to visit a second time when school is in session.

Talk to anyone who has visited numerous colleges and s/he will tell you how tiring the visits are. I am not sure why the visits seem so exhausting, but trust me, they are. Perhaps, it is all the thinking or the emotion of considering the next life step for both the parents and the students. As you plan, include time for driving, resting, eating and sleeping. I have found that an average of 1.5 visits per day suits me and my students just fine. That means that you can plan on three visits in two days. The marathon of ten schools in a week is killer!

PREPARING FOR YOUR CAMPUS VISIT

This heading certainly sounds like work, doesn't it? But, yes, you should prepare for your visit ahead of time. So, how do you prepare for a college visit? I recommend several steps:

1. **Research**: Don't worry. This is not a research paper; it's just a chance for you to get to know the colleges better. You should plan on spending 30 minutes or so online at the prospective college's

website. A good place to start is the College "Viewbook" essentially its advertising brochure. Does the brochure focus equally or appropriately on academics, athletics, music and arts and other activities? Next, visit the admissions office. Take a look at the undergraduate admissions application. Is there anything outstanding on the application? Read about how the admissions decisions are made; often colleges will list the importance of:

- Grades
- Board Scores (ACT/SAT)
- Course Rigor
- Extracurricular Activities

If you are sure of your major, make sure the college offers it under the "Academics" link. Search for the course catalog. Do the courses interest you? Does anything jump out at you? Make a note of any questions that you have.

Why do you have to do all this? First, it will give you a much better understanding of the school and will make your visit more productive as you will already have a context for considering the school. Second, it will prepare you to ask questions and gain more insight or knowledge or data in the information session, tour and interview. Third, preparation will give you credibility with the admissions office. If you have an interview or group session, the preparation will help you greatly. Finally, some schools have little contests in which they ask prospective students trivia questions about their school. You may even win a t-shirt or a key chain. See, preparation can really pay off!

2. **Print out the application:** You don't have to complete the application, but do make note of its requirements. Some schools will offer an instant admission at a college visit. If this is the case, it should be noted under the admissions tab on the college's website. Wouldn't

it be nice to have an acceptance in your back pocket the same day that you visit the school?

3. **Organize your file box with:**

- Transcript - unofficial is fine for a visit. Official transcripts can be sent from your high school

- Copies of your SAT/ACT scores online print outs are fine for the visits; you will need to send score reports from CollegeBoard.org or ACT.org when you apply

- Several copies of your student resume

- Several copies of your athletic/arts/music resume, if applicable

- Your portfolio, if applicable

DRESSING FOR SUCCESS

Recently, I embarked on a college visit trip in South Carolina and Georgia. It seemed like a good idea to bring my 16-year old daughter with me. Even though the schools that I intended to visit did not really meet Emma's needs, I thought that it would be a learning experience for her as she was finishing her sophomore year. Our first stop was The Citadel, a very formal military college in Charleston, South Carolina. The night before, the ten-hour drive had turned into a sixteen-hour drive through torrential thunderstorms. Our GPS, who goes by the name of "Hildegard", seemed absolutely determined to drive us into a median, through a guardrail or a barrier wall; every time we refused, she had to "recalculate." If you have a GPS, you know what I mean.

Arriving at the hotel in the middle of the night was an incredible relief. As a college coach, I was smart enough to make sure to have the file tote ready with Emma's resume, her preliminary test scores and transcript. As a mother, it did not occur to me to ask Emma what she intended to wear to this MILITARY institute. And to make matters worse, my husband had somehow left my suitcase at home, so I could not even lend her anything.

The morning of our visit, I scrounged in my overnight bag to see if I could cobble together something appropriate to wear on a college tour and interview. When I lifted my head from the minimal depths of the tiny little bag, I laid eyes on my daughter in a micro-mini black dress with a plunging neckline, held together with safety pins the size of diaper pins. Did I handle the situation with calm and good judgment? No, way! I screeched, "You are not wearing THAT to The Citadel!" After several, "Moms," dragged into two syllables, "Mo-om", Emma decided that it was not worth fighting with the crazy woman. She consented to change. Next thing I knew, she was in a similarly horrid outfit, this time with a slinky, shiny blouse and awful black pin-striped "dress" pants with a ripped hem. Well, you can imagine that things did not get better from there. "You are NOT wearing that, either." Emma's response, "Well, I have a 'Brew-Thru' shirt." Don't even ask me what a 'Brew-Thru' shirt is.

In the end, Emma wore the slinky shirt and awful pants. As is befitting, The Citadel Admissions Office was ready for Emma's tour and interview. The secretary did say something along the lines of "Welcome, Emma. Gee, you sure don't look like most of the students that come to visit us." Of course, the other students who come to visit are prepared ahead of time with a decent outfit! So, I learned a lesson and can share it with you.

Remember that your college visit is similar to a job interview. You do not have to wear a suit and tie or a dress, but you do have to step up from grunge. A good idea is khakis and a polo shirt with comfortable shoes, but not flip-flops. If it is really hot out, you can get away with clean, preferably ironed, long shorts.

WHAT TO EXPECT WHEN YOU VISIT

I like to break visits into two categories: large schools and small schools. If you are visiting a large school, plan on signing into the admissions office. Try to arrive early enough to request the business card for the admissions officer assigned to your state/region. You may be asked to fill out an information sheet for the college's database. At the appointed time, you will most likely enter an auditorium or other large room for the admissions officer presentation. This presentation is usually conducted by an admissions officer with the help of a Power Point presentation. Sometimes current college students will take part in the presentation as well. After the formal presentation is completed, the admissions officer will take questions from the audience. Between the presentation and question and answer session, you will learn a lot. Feel free to interject your own questions, if they have not already been answered.

Once all the questions are answered, a group of student tour guides will introduce themselves. They will separate the audience into groups of ten to twenty people for tours and then take off in different directions. Sometimes, tours will be divided randomly and other times by majors or interests.

If you are visiting a small school (2500 or fewer students), you may be surprised at the reception that you will receive. When you arrive on campus, head for the admissions office. Often right outside the office, you will see a portable sign that says welcome, "Your Name". The schools may only have two or three visitors each day. Like at larger schools, you will be asked to fill out a questionnaire. Ask for the business card of the admissions officer for your region so that you can write a thank you note upon your return home. Most small schools will start with a personal interview. Parents may be included or may not be. There is more information on interviewing below so don't stress out. The colleges want to impress you as much as you want to impress them.

After your interview or small group information session, you can expect a tour. Often it will be a private tour for just you and your family. If this is the case, be aware that the tour guide is observing you and will write up his/her observations of you on his/her return to the admissions office. Be on good behavior!

TAKING NOTES WHEN YOU VISIT

You should always take some notes when you visit a college. Buy a spiral notebook and keep track of your impressions. It will help you to remember specifics later when you are getting ready to apply.

WHAT TO ASK THE ADMISSIONS OFFICER

You should ask the admissions officer any appropriate questions that come to mind. If the information is most likely available on the website or in the admissions literature, make sure to do that research early. You will sound silly asking CalPoly if they offer an engineering degree! I have listed some questions to get you started:

1. What is your average class size for freshmen and sophomores?

2. What is your average class size for upperclassmen?

3. Are all of your class taught by professors or do teaching assistants conduct classes and labs also?

4. What percentage of students receive financial aid/merit aid?

5.   What are the criteria for your admissions decisions?

6.   How would you describe your ideal college applicant?

7.   What is the retention rate from freshman to sophomore years?

8.   What is the retention rate from freshman to senior years?

9.   What percentage of students completes their undergraduate work in four years?

10.   What percentage of students continues to graduate school?

11.   What career counseling and placement services does the college offer?

12.   How does the administration handle alcohol and drug infractions?

13.   Is there an honor code and how does it work?

14.   Does the college have an emergency protocol for natural disasters, campus intruder, etc?

15.   Is there a campus security service?

WHAT TO ASK YOUR STUDENT TOUR GUIDE

While your student tour guide is essentially an employee of the college, the more casual tour will give you an opportunity to not only see the campus, but also to pick the brain of a real live student. These questions can be more open-ended than those for the admissions officers. Start by getting to know the tour guide. Some softball questions will help to open the conversation. Remember, your goal is not to intimidate or box in the tour guide. S/he may not know the answers to all your questions. You also do not have to ask all of these sample questions below. They are just to get you thinking:

1. What year are you?

2. Did you start here as a freshman?

3. If not, where did you go before?

4. What other colleges did you consider?

5. Why did you choose to come here?

6. What do you like about this school? (You can ask what s/he does not like, but a savvy tour guide will sidestep that question).

7. How's the workload?

8. How much do you study?

9. Where do you study?

10. How often do you go home?

11. Was it hard getting used to being away from home?

12. What are the professors like?

13. Do you have a favorite professor?

14. Do you feel like you are getting a good education?

15. Is college a lot harder than high school?

16. What will you do after you graduate?

17. How's the food?

18. Do you live in a dorm now?

19. How did you pick your roommate and dorm first year?

20. What happens if you get sick?

21. Does the campus have good security?

22. Do you always feel safe here?

23. Who teaches your classes?

24. Do you ever have teaching assistants?

25. What about online classes?

26. What is your average class size?

27. Do most students live on campus or close-by in apartments, etc.?

28. Do lots of students leave campus on weekends?

29. What do students do for fun?

30. Do you have Greeks (fraternities and sororities)?

31. How many students are in fraternities and sororities?

32. Do a lot of students participate in sports?

33. Would you recommend this school for your younger brother or sister?

34. How does the school handle alcohol and drug infractions?

35. Is the honor code fair and balanced?

INTERVIEWING ON-AND OFF-CAMPUS

Most of the large universities no longer take the time to conduct individual interviews. In general, small and private schools provide opportunities for students to interview with an admissions officer or with an alumni representative locally. Make sure to prepare for the interview ahead of time as you would for a college visit.

If you are interviewing on-campus at the college, it is smart to attend the admissions information session and to take the campus tour with the student guide before your interview to develop a better understanding of the school. Since you will be walking a good bit before an on-campus interview, you will need to wear comfortable shoes and clothes. Nevertheless, you do not want to dress so casually as to appear less than serious. Remember that you are visiting a professional office where people do not wear flip-flops or shorts! Plan ahead to have enough time for the tour and to then find the appropriate building and office for the interview. You do not want to be late!!

If you are interviewing with a local admissions or alumni representative, the same rules apply. Make sure to dress appropriately and arrive on time for your interview.

Bring a copy of your student resume, transcript and SAT/ACT score reports. Develop questions ahead of time. Think about your skills, strengths and weaknesses, favorite classes, books, etc., so that you may answer these basic questions with ease. Answer all questions honestly, without embellishment. Ask for the interviewer's business card before leaving and make absolutely sure to write a thank you note within two to three days of the visit. This correspondence will go in your application folder and may even end up as a deciding factor in the admissions decision. Remember, colleges and universities want to know that you are truly interested in their programs and that there is a good possibility that you will attend, if accepted.

College interviews are not like what you may have seen in the movies. The college's motivation for interviewing is to really get to know students. They do not want to terrorize you. Most of the questions will be easy and conversational. You do have to prepare, but don't drive yourself nuts. Remember to shake the interviewer's hand upon meeting him/her and to introduce your parents. Once you are in the interview room, offer your student resume, transcript and board scores. This organization will give you big brownie points with the admissions officer.

INTERVIEW QUESTIONS

Two of the most important questions in a college interview are:

1. Tell me about yourself?

You should have a 90-120 second response prepared for this question. Think about who you are and what you represent. You do not want to regurgitate your student resume, but your answer should reflect the same person that is on the paper.

2. Why do you want to attend this college?

This is where your research is going to pay off. If you are unable to answer this question substantively, you will give the impression of being another desperate kid hoping to get accepted somewhere, maybe anywhere.

Other questions include:

1. What do you like about our university?
2. What sets you apart from the other kajillion kids applying to college?
3. What do you want to study and why?
4. Where do you see yourself in five, ten years?
5. What has been your favorite high school class and why?
6. What has been your least favorite high school class and why?
7. Tell me about a time when you had to resolve a difficult personal issue or overcome an obstacle.
8. How will you bring diversity to our university?
9. Where else are you applying?
10. Have you thought about studying abroad or graduate school?

DON'T DO ANYTHING STUPID!

This is one of my favorite categories. You probably remember this from other sections of the book. So, when you are visiting colleges, don't do anything stupid! How do I define stupid? Well, it goes on a scale from dumb to truly idiotic!:

1. First, make sure to visit any and all schools with an open mind. If you really don't think that you will like a specific school because you have heard rumors from other kids or know someone that did not like the school, try to be open-minded for just a little while. See what the school has to offer and if anything piques your interest. Remember that you may find things about a specific school that you like and want to remember for other visits.

2. Don't dress like Emma did at The Citadel.

3. Don't wear clothes or logos from another college.

4. Remember that you are being observed by the college staff. Do not take this opportunity to give your little brother a noogie, roll your eyes at your parents or worse.

5. Even if you are in a really bad mood, tired or otherwise out-of-sorts, try to remain positive. You have a great opportunity when visiting colleges.

6. This might seem obvious, but do not argue or correct your tour guide. S/he may make errors; you are not the one to correct him/her or anyone else on campus!

"ROMANCING" THE ADMISSIONS OFFICER

What a strange heading, *Romancing the Admissions Officer*! Many students set their hearts on one college or university as the one and only school for themselves. Usually, this one school is just a bit out of reach. Why do some of these very same students find themselves accepted to their dream school and others do not? The difference is often in the student's approach to the admissions office.

Some colleges actually keep track of the number of times that a student visits their university, attends local presentations, and even takes advantage of school information sessions. According to the admissions offices, this data collection helps the admissions officers to measure a student's commitment and thus, potential, to attend their university. It is very important to always sign in to any presentation, tour, information session, and even to college nights at the local high school or mall. Make sure that whenever possible, you attend local open houses, College Nights/Fairs and stop by the school Career Center when any of the colleges on your short list visit your school. Remember Grace Bennington's experience, with the president of her choice school (described in Chapter 4).

When you are working your way through this process, remember to put yourself in the college admissions officers' shoes. They see hundreds, if not thousands, of applications each year. Large universities may receive 20,000, 30,000 or more applications. Imagine that amount of paper and data! It becomes an exhausting blur. The more that you can do to develop a relationship and put your qualifications and personality in front of the admissions officer, the better off you will be. While you do not want to bother the admissions officer, I have found that they are very open to receiving phone calls and emails that share information.

Once you have fallen in love with a college, let the admissions officer know. Write a reasonably effusive thank-you note. Keep in touch with the admissions officer for your area by email. As you finish your junior year and are choosing classes, consult with the admissions officer about final choices for your senior year. If you plan to visit the school again or to stay overnight with a student, let the admissions officer know. Forward your SAT/ACT/AP/IB scores to the admissions officer. Share your first quarter grades. When emailing, it is a good idea to strike up a conversation and set the email up to require a response by asking questions. Generally, the more interest you show, the more interest the college will have in you (as long as the academic match is reasonable)!!

EXPLAINING DIFFICULT TIMES, LOWER GRADES AND SAT/ACT SCORES

Many students experience times of difficulty during their four years of high school. Sometimes, these difficulties lead to lower grades or board scores. While colleges do not want to hear sob stories, they do want to know about your special circumstances that explain a decline in your grades, attendance, SAT/ACT scores, etc. Some examples include: major illness, significant family change (job loss, move, death), learning disability, school change, or social event (bullying, intimidation).

If you have suffered a difficult circumstance, it is important to let your prospective colleges know. It is also important to use the utmost care in sharing your information. Below, are two written explanations that Professional Tutoring students have provided to colleges. As you will see, neither of the students feels sorry for himself; they explain the situation and also indicate how they overcame the obstacle. Both students also talk about how the difficult circumstance has led to personal growth and maturity, thus furthering their attractiveness to colleges. The colleges want mature, prepared students. Students who have never had to face any difficulties may really struggle in college as they face the beginnings of adult life.

The first example below is part of a student resume; note that the asterisk by the grades refers the reader to a third page addendum.

GPA: 9th: 3.4   11th: 3.4

10th: 2.8*   12th: 3.4

*Statement of Explanation for Grades in Sophomore Year"

In my sophomore year my family moved for one year to Montgomery, Alabama. In that year, I was the target of significant hazing and discrimination at my private school. I was harassed, bullied and physically threatened by a group of students. My locker was vandalized with curse words three times; students threw ice at me when I was cheering during pep rallies and a few very mean-spirited girls started untrue rumors about me on a regular basis. I had very few friends, and became depressed. The teachers and counselors did not know me since I was new, so it took time for them to realize how far from the truth these allegations were. I later found out that the main reason all the bullying began was that a few of the girls saw my Facebook from my former school and saw that a close male friend was African-American. The girls thought he was my boyfriend, so I was labeled with a hateful slur word for the rest of the year.

My parents considered taking me out of the school, but since we were only there for one year, it seemed like the best thing was to try and stick it out. The principal intervened on my behalf, and I finished the year. Despite my low GPA for this year, I actually learned a lot from the experience. I had always been part of the "in crowd" but for that one year, I was the kid who did not fit in. As a result, I am even more friendly and open to people around me who are a little different or who happen to be new.

The second example is a well-written personal narrative. In this narrative, the student talks about working with and overcoming his learning disability. Again, this young man is explaining his obstacle without feeling sorry for himself. He also turns the hardship into a growing and learning experience.

"That which does not kill you makes you stronger," said our great leader, President Franklin Delano Roosevelt, while the United States was in the midst of the Great Depression. Our nation endured that terrible time, recovering in the advent of the "war to end all wars." Our nation is built on overcoming obstacles, creating new solutions, and marching forward. As an American by birth and a patriotic and loyal citizen, I have taken FDR's great words to heart. While few daily occurrences intimidate me, sometimes the simplest of assignments can frustrate me to no end.

"Take out a sheet of paper, we are going to take notes" -- my least favorite phrase. I have a learning disability (auditory memory), and notes are probably the hardest thing for me. People all around me are scribbling, penciling away, and I sit nearly paralyzed, stuck on the bit about getting out paper.

Over the years I have had to work around my learning disability. Although I have had an Individualized Educational Plan (IEP) since second grade, I have consistently worked to overcome my disability and not to use my IEP as a crutch. I used to hide my disability from my friends; I thought they would make fun of me because I could not do things as fast. I sometimes became frustrated with how much faster others learned. Freshman year, I had an epiphany. I came to realize that hard work and determination could push me beyond the challenges of my learning disability. My grades increased rapidly, from the low 3.0 range to almost a 4.0. I realized that my disability did not have to hold me back and that I did not need the accommodations in the IEP as others had thought. I began using time management skills; I know exactly how long it takes me to do almost any kind of work. I have taken my work to the next level and have begun to time myself on how fast I work and what kind of grades I earn. After I get the timing down, I work as hard as I could to speed up my times.

Last year, my skills really came together. I found that at this new peak I could take notes easily. My grades shot up. My writing dramatically improved. Studying definitely worked. At the beginning of the year, I scored below 1000 on a practice SAT Reasoning Exam. By the end of the year I had a 1700. The time and determination paid off and have prepared me for the next step: my senior year and college.

I used to think of my disability as something that crippled me. Now, I know what it really is--a blessing in disguise. Rather than being a weight on my shoulders, my disability has actually turned out to be a benefit, for it has forced me to work harder and more efficiently than most. I would not trade it for anything; it makes me who I am. FDR was right: adversity makes us stronger

FINAL DECISIONS

In the spring of your senior year, you will be making your final college decision. With good planning, you should have several acceptances from schools in which you are truly interested. If you have not visited any of the schools on your short-list of consideration, make sure to set up a campus tour, one or two class visits and an overnight stay with a student in the dorms. It is important to try to spend at least one night at the school so that you get a real insider's perspective. You will be spending four years at this school; it is crucial that you look into every nook and cranny of the campus to make sure that you will fit into the school academically and socially.

If you have important non-negotiable criteria on your list, such as whether all students have guaranteed housing (some schools do not even guarantee housing for incoming freshmen), whether students are allowed to have cars on campus, etc., make sure to check out these issues BEFORE you apply. Before making the final decision, make sure that your financial aid package is finalized.

Finally, remember to accept or decline all of your offers graciously. Once you have made your decision (with your parents) and sent in the requisite deposits, write to the other schools which accepted you. Thank them for their consideration and politely decline their offers.

NOTES

_____

_____

_____

_____

_____

_____

_____

_____

Chapter 9

Specialized Applications

· ·

Specialized Applications include specific processes for military (Reserve Officer Training Corps and the U.S. Service Academies), music, arts and athletic programs. These specialized programs require expertise to stand out in a field of talent. Continue reading to learn about the process.

RESERVE OFFICER TRAINING CORPS

The Reserve Officer Training Corps (ROTC) offers students the opportunity to prepare for a career as a United States military officer while attending a civilian college. The ROTC program is considered a college elective and requires approximately several dedicated hours per week in the classroom and in other drills. Many students choose to consider the ROTC program for its major scholarship programs.

IN THIS CHAPTER

• Learn the requirements for ROTC programs and how to apply to the five U.S. Service Academies

• Read a winning letter of recommendation to the U.S. Naval Academy

• Learn how to write an Athletic or Music Resume

The scholarship programs require at least four years of active military duty after graduating/commissioning. All three programs have specific grade and board score standards. The ROTC requires a separate application, interview and recommendations. Students should begin this process by the summer before senior year. In addition to applying to the ROTC program, you must apply and gain admission to the specific college(s) at which you want to participate in ROTC.

Not all colleges have ROTC programs. Some colleges "share" programs; students from other local colleges may participate in their programs. By far, Army has the largest program, Air Force the second, and Navy the third. Most Marine recruits come from the Navy ROTC program. The basic requirements for each program are below. If you are interested in applying for the ROTC programs, make sure to visit the websites:

Army ROTC: armyrotc.com

Navy ROTC: nrotc.navy.mil

Air Force ROTC: afrotc.com

The information included here has been gleaned from the three websites listed above; it is correct to the best of my knowledge; you should verify the information with your own research.

Air Force ROTC:

The U.S. Air Force offers three and four year scholarships of up to full college tuition, "most" fees and $900 per year. In addition, the Air Force allocates a nontaxable monthly stipend of $300 to $500 during the academic year.

The Air Force has two programs. The first, General Military Course (GMC) is available to freshmen and sophomores who meet the following requirements:

- United States Citizen (if on scholarship)

- Good physical condition

- Good moral character

- Age 14 years or older (17 years old to receive a scholarship)

- The U.S. Air Force website also lists disqualifying attributes

The U.S. Air Force ROTC Professional Officer Course (POC) is available to college juniors and seniors who meet the following qualifications:

- United States Citizen

- Be of legal age (set by individual states) or 17 years old with a parent/guardian's consent

- Be in good academic standing

- 4-year and 2-year Program: have two academic years remaining in a degree program (undergraduate, graduate or both)

- Participate in both Aerospace Studies class and Leadership Laboratory each semester

- Meet physical requirements

Army ROTC:

The Army ROTC program offers two, three and four-year scholarship programs of up to full tuition. The Army ROTC programs may also provide an allowance for books and additional college fees. Like the Air Force ROTC, Army ROTC provides a $300 to $500 stipend per month.

The U.S. Army ROTC program has the following requirements:

- United States Citizenship
- Be between the ages of 17 and 26
- High school GPA of at least 2.5
- High school diploma or equivalent
- SAT minimum score of 920 (Reading and Math)
- ACT minimum score of 19 (excluding writing)
- Meet physical standards

Navy ROTC:

The third ROTC program, Navy ROTC, offers scholarship programs similar to those of Air Force and Army ROTC programs. The Navy ROTC scholarship will cover up to $180,000 of tuition, books and related college expenses at 160 colleges and universities. The Navy ROTC program also offers the monthly stipend.

The U.S. Navy ROTC program has the following requirements:

- United States Citizenship
- Be between the ages of 17 and 23
- High school diploma or equivalent
- SAT minimum score of 530 Critical Reading, 520 Math
- ACT minimum score of 21 Math, 22 English
- Board scores may be waived in favor of top 10% class rank
- Meet physical standards
- Morality clause (see website)

SERVICE ACADEMIES

The United States has five service academies including:

1. The U.S. Military Academy at West Point, NY (usma.edu)

2. The U.S. Naval Academy at Annapolis, MD (usna.edu)

3. The United States Air Force Academy at Colorado Springs, CO (usafa.edu)

4. The United States Coast Guard Academy at New London, CT (cga.edu)

5. United States Merchant Marine Academy at Kings Point, NY (usmma.edu)

The Service Academies generally look for top students and athletes with high integrity and leadership abilities who will commit themselves to a career as military officers. The appointment and admissions process is more complicated than that of the average American college/university. If you are interested in one of the academies, begin research early (by the spring of the junior year). The best place to start is the individual websites. If accepted to a United States Service Academy, be prepared to pay NO tuition/room and board/fees. Your commitment to four years of undergraduate work and five years of post-graduate service as a military, Merchant Marine or Coast Guard officer covers the costs of your college education. Estimates of the value of this four year education range from $200,000 to $300,000.

All of the service academies, except for the U.S. Coast Guard Academy, require a Congressional or Executive nomination for appointment. Surprisingly, there is not a standardized nominating procedure. Each Congressional office has the discretion to develop its own procedure for its limited number of possible appointments. In addition to Senators and Representatives, members of the Executive Branch, including the President, Vice President, Secretaries of the Army, Navy and Air Force, Service Academy Superintendent, Governor of Puerto Rico and Resident Representative, Commonwealth of the Northern Mariana Island, may also make appointments. If you are interested in requesting a nomination to one of the U.S. Service Academies, contact your Senator or Representative's offices of the office(s) of the Executive Branch listed above.

In addition to seeking nomination, you must meet the requirements of the individual Service Academies. Each academy will have its own process; all five require an initial application to begin the application process. To apply to one of the U.S. Service Academies, applicants must meet the following criteria set by law:

- American Citizen
- Between 17 and 22 years of age by July 1 before entering the Academy (USMA, USNA, USCGA, USAFA). The age limit for the USMMA is 25 years
- Unmarried
- Not pregnant and without legal obligation to support children or other dependents

In addition to these statutory requirements, qualified Service Academy candidates will:

- Demonstrate comprehensive academic preparation
- Demonstrate leadership in athletics and other extracurricular activities
- Provide SAT Reasoning Exam and/or ACT Exam scores

- Be in good physical and mental health
- Pass a comprehensive medical examination
- Pass a physical aptitude examination

In seeking a nomination to a U.S. Service Academy, expect to prepare the following documents for your intended Senator, Member of Congress or of the Executive Branch:

1. A nomination application (request or download from Congressional or Executive websites)
2. Official high school transcripts
3. Official copy of your SAT Reasoning and/or SAT scores
4. Two to three letters of recommendation from teachers, coaches, employers, community members, as specified on the nomination request form

In applying to one of the U.S. Service Academies, you are seeking to represent the United States as an Army, Navy, Air Force, Merchant Marine or Coast Guard officer. As such, the application review process will be both more stringent and holistic than most colleges. Expect to interview repeatedly. You will be evaluated on your:

- Academics
- Leadership
- Character
- Physical Aptitude; and Medical Fitness

I am including a recommendation letter that I wrote several years ago for an outstanding applicant to the U.S. Naval Academy. In the letter, you will notice the focus on Ben's character. Remember that a good recommendation will reinforce the applicant's attributes with specific examples and evidence. Ben was admitted to the U.S. Naval Academy at Annapolis. He is now a midshipman.

*** Source for information on U.S. Service Academies: (SOURCE: Congressional Research Service, February 21, 2006 by R. Eric Petersen)

Professional Tutoring, LLC
11901 Cub Court
Fairfax Station, VA 22039
703.830.7037
professionaltutoring@cox.net
www.juliarossprofessionaltutoring.com

Dean of Admissions
United States Naval Academy
117 Decatur Road
Annapolis, MD 21402-9978

Dear Sir or Madam:

It is a pleasure to recommend Mr. Benjamin Smith for admission to the United States Naval Academy. In the past year that I have worked with Ben as both a teacher and employer, I have been very impressed with him.

Ben sought my tutelage services during his junior year and enrolled in a pre-calculus course. After a couple of sessions, Ben was able to catch up with the class. Ben consistently sought a deeper understanding of this gateway to higher mathematics. He asked searching questions, looking for the theory behind the math; I often had to consult additional resources to answer his questions.

Once Ben had finished his junior year and enrolled in calculus for twelfth grade, he began my Scholastic Aptitude Test (SAT) preparation course for seniors. Again, Ben's thirst for knowledge surfaced. His native intelligence allows him to understand many, many concepts at a more profound level than most people. The challenge with Ben in a classroom is meeting and directing his very strong abilities while also providing for the needs of the more average students. It is for this reason that Ben belongs at a superior university.

Earlier this fall, I asked Ben to work as an assistant tutor to support another professional tutor during my maternity leave in February. Ben's strong math skills and Spanish fluency made him an obvious choice to support the academic needs of my regular students.

In addition, I chose Ben because of his strong social skills, leadership ability and reliability.

In September, I unexpectedly needed to cover an eight-hour tutoring day. I called Ben at the very last minute. He made arrangements and appeared at my door early, prepared to work all day. With an adult tutor and another assistant, Ben worked with groups of students. He covered several subjects at once, moving between students, teaching math, history, English, Spanish and physics seamlessly. With no preparation, Ben was able to provide appropriate direction and support to other young people, often of his own age. Ben consistently broke assignments and concepts into manageable steps appropriate to each student's needs and level.

At the end of the day, I prepared to compensate Ben as we had agreed. He deferred, saying that he would like to offer service hours for this first session. I was shocked and tried to convince him to accept at least partial payment. He refused politely, saying that he had enjoyed the day and would accept payment in the winter. Although many students have service hour requirements, this occasion went above and beyond service hours. Ben had worked as a professional adult in an environment that would challenge any student. Again, my level of respect for Ben rose. The other student who had assisted during the day chimed in with, "He may not want to be paid, but I do Mrs. Ross!" While this certainly broke the ice, it underlined Ben's ethics and character.

Ben is a very mature young man. Not only gifted academically and athletically, he has an outstanding character. I would recommend him to the USNA without hesitation. Our country should be honored to have Ben Smith serve us.

Sincerely,

Julia Ross, Owner

ATHLETICS

There are quite a few options for college sports. The two major athletic organizations are the NCAA and NAIA. These are the organizations that will offer scholarships and recruit athletes. The college athlete's experience will center around athletics with many hours of practice each week. In addition to intercollegiate athletics, many colleges and universities offer less competitive club teams.

1. NCAA: "The National Collegiate Athletic Association (NCAA) is a voluntary organization through which the nation's colleges and universities govern their athletic programs. It is comprised of institutions, conferences, organizations and individuals committed to the best interests, education and athletics participation of student-athletes." (NCAA.com) The NCAA represents over 1200 colleges and 380,000 student athletes. Within the NCAA, there are three athletic divisions, NCAA I, II and III. The NCAA I division is the most competitive. Generally, the NCAA I division is made up of the largest universities. Division I and II colleges are allowed to offer athletic scholarships. While Division III schools do not offer financial assistance to athletes, many will offer other types of merit scholarships to athletes whom they wish to attract.

In order to be considered for college athletics, you must register with the NCAA Clearinghouse. The NCAA has very specific rules regarding contracts between college coaches and athletes. Be sure to read these rules carefully before taking even the first step into the competitive college athletic recruitment process (www. NCAAClearinghouse.net).

2. NAIA: National Association of Intercollegiate Athletics is another voluntary organization of colleges and athletes. Smaller than the NCAA, its membership includes just under 300 colleges and universities in the United States and Canada. The NAIA has several different policies than the NCAA for membership and recruitment.

3. Working with the Coaches: As mentioned above, the college athletic associations have very specific governing rules regarding coach/ high school athlete interaction. Your first step should be with your own high school or club coach. Your high school/club coach will have the best idea of your abilities and potential. This coach will serve as the liaison between the athlete and college coaches. It will be important during your high school athletic career to keep track of your statistics, awards, and team records. Often the next step will be to have yourself filmed in your sport.

4. **Athletic Resumes:** A sample format and Allison Leigh's athletic resume follow:

Great Athlete
11901 Cub Court
Fairfax Station, VA 22039
greatestathlete@msn.com

Personal:
Age: Height: Weight: Sport(s):

Education:
School & District: Graduation Date:
GPA:
SAT/ACT:
NCAA Status: Registration date with NCAA Clearinghouse

High School Sports Statistics:
Team Name:
Position:
9th Grade:
10th Grade:
11th Grade:
12th Grade:

Community Sports Statistics:

Team Name:

Position:
9th Grade: 11th Grade
10th Grade: 12th Grade

Athletic Honors/Awards:

Other Sports:
Mention other sports

Specialized Sports Training:
Camps, Clinics, Summer, Leagues, Volunteer Positions, etc.

References:
Coach, Team Name: E-Mail, Phone Number

Attachments:
News articles, coaches' letters of recommendation, training evaluations, film (DVD)

Allison Leigh
59875 Shadow Lane
Springfield, Virginia 22151
(777) 555-6490 allison.leigh@studentmail.edu

PERSONAL
D.O.B: December 19, 1990
Parents: Jim & Alicia Leigh
Hobbies: Physical fitness, reading, babysitting
Height. & Weight: 5'1", 110 lbs
Sports: Lacrosse and Soccer

ACADEMICS

Wheatfield High School: 6100 Rolling Rd, Springfield. VA 22152. Class of 2009. Guidance Counselor: Sarah Vink – email address
GPA: 2.60   SAT: 1420

Community Service: Christie's Christmas (2007-pres), Eddie's Club (2005-'07), Beautification Day (2008), Lacrosse Outreach (2007-pres)

Extracurricular Activities: Key Club (2006-2009), Hometown Vet Clinic (2007-2008)

ATHLETICS

Soccer Clubs:
    Springfield Youth Club Rec League (1999–2003)
    Washington Area Girls Soccer (WAGS) SYC
    Xplosion DIV: Starting Ctr-mid (2004-07)

High School Lacrosse:
    Freshman: JV Starting Attack (2006)
    Sophomore: JV Starting Attack (Captain) (2007)
    Junior: Varsity-Starting 3rd Man Defense (2008)
    Senior: Varsity Starting Defense (Captain) (2009)

Recruited: Guest Player: WAGS SYC Galaxy DII Center Mid
WAGS SYC Xplosion P.W. Cty Labor Day Tourn. (2008)

SPECIALIZED SPORTS TRAINING:

Givargas (GIVA) Soccer Camp Sweet Briar (2005)
Longwood U. Lacrosse Camp ('06)
Woodson Fall-Ball (2007-present)
Winter Conditioning (2007-pres.)
Metro Summer League (2008-present)
Turkey Tournament (2007-present)
Valentine's Day Shoot-out (Valentine's 2007-present)

AWARDS/HONORS:
9th – 10th grade: Junior Varsity Lacrosse High Scorer
11th grade: Varsity Lacrosse Letter

REFERENCES:

Joe Wendlberger: Xplosion and Galaxie Head
Coach: email address and phone

Brian Puhlick: Varsity Lacrosse Head
Coach: email address and phone

Jill Marvin: Varsity Lacrosse Assistant
Coach: email address and phone

MUSIC, FINE ARTS & THEATER:

Like athletics, the arts have a special place in the university community. If you have a special interest in the arts, you will want to begin your portfolio, repertoire, etc., by the middle of your junior year.

As with athletics, the teachers will play an integral role in your interaction with the universities. Art students will need to develop a portfolio in different media. Music students should keep track of the pieces that you have performed and practiced. Music students should make CD's and/or DVD's of their performances. Theater students also need to keep track of their performances.

By the end of the junior year, music, fine arts and theater students should be making contacts with appropriate offices in the university. The admissions office is often a good first stop. Also, your coaches/teachers will help make initial contacts.

Music Student
Street Address
City State, Zip
Phone
Student#4@verizon.net

Activities: For the past ten years I have been taking piano lessons. Two years ago, I began taking lessons at the Levine School of Music in Washington, D.C. Levine School is accredited by the National Association of Schools of Music and has given me many opportunities for performance. There is mandatory jury twice a year, and emphasis on technique and interpretation. I love to play the piano, whether I am playing for myself or others. Piano has given me the opportunity to display my leadership qualities through performing for church, junior church, and chapel services. I have also been a member of the yearbook staff since my freshman year. To be a member of the staff, a student must be invited by an upperclassman and the invitation must be approved by the faculty advisor.

Awards: My freshman year I received the Christian Character Award. At the end of the school year, this honor is awarded by the faculty of Fairfax Baptist Temple Academy to a high school student who demonstrates Christian character and an aptitude for leadership. A student is eligible to receive this award once during his/her academic career at Fairfax Baptist Temple Academy.

Music Competitions: The Old Dominion Association of Church Schools is an organization of church school ministries throughout the commonwealth of Virginia. About 5,300 students from 46 schools make up the ODACS family. The highlight of each year is the ODACS Bible, Fine Arts, and Academic Competition. Students compete on elementary, junior high and senior high levels in over 150 categories. Areas of competition include Bible, vocal and instrumental music, speech, art, and academic testing. In March of 2007, over 3,500 students competed at the regional competitions, and over 800 students competed at the annual state competition.

Service Activities: For the past year I have been accompanying the Junior Church at Fairfax Baptist Temple and will continue to accompany them this fall. All through high school, I have been the substitute pianist for chapel services. As the substitute I was expected to fill in at the last minute when necessary. Beginning my senior year I will be the first pianist for all high school chapel services.

Available for Review: Portfolio, DVD/still photographs of work/concerts, letters of recommendation from specialized teachers/coaches, repertoire list.

MUSIC EXPERIENCE

2006
- Classical Piano Solo: Placed 1st Regional with Sonata No. 8 Op. 13, Beethoven

2007
- Classical Piano Solo: Placed 1st Regional and 2nd State with Polonaise in A Major, Chopin
- Music Theory Testing: Placed 1st Regional and 2nd State
- Senior High Hand Bell Choir: Placed 1st at Regional and 2nd at State

2008
- Classical Piano Solo
- Music Theory Testing
- Senior High Hand Bell Choir

Piano Accompaniment: Piano accompaniment has given me the opportunity to display my leadership qualities and has challenged me to balance academics, music, and social activities. I have learned to manage my time very well. Following are the groups I have had the opportunity to participate with as piano accompaniment:

2004 -2005
- Kindergarten Choir

2005 - 2006
- Junior High Choir

2006 - 2007
- Small Instrumental Ensemble
- High School Orchestra
- High School Choir
- Jr. Church
- School Chapel Service

2007 - 2008
- Small Instrumental Ensemble
- High School Orchestra
- Jr. Church
- School Chapel Services

Music Student: Repertoire List

Night in Tunisia:	Dizzy Gillespie
Wind Machine:	Sammy Nestico
Autumn Leaves:	Joseph Kosma
Take the A Train:	Billy Strayhorn
Tune-Up:	Miles Davis
Impressions:	John Coltrane
Little Sunflower:	Freddie Hubbard
Blue Bossa:	Kenny Durham
So What:	Miles Davis
Four:	Miles Davis
Impressions:	John Coltrane
Misty:	Earl Garner
Unit 7:	Sam Jones
Sun Down:	Wes Montgomery
Wave:	Antonio Carlos Job
Manah de Carnival:	Luis Bonfa
Sonny Moon for Two:	Sonny Rollins
Cantelope Island:	Herbie Hancock
Chitlins Con Carne:	Kenny Barell
Billie's Bounce:	Charlie Parker
Now's The Time:	Charlie Parker
Fried Pies:	Wes Montgomery
Satin Doll:	Duke Ellington
Summertime:	George Gershwin
Afternoon in Paris:	John Lewis
All Blues:	Miles Davis
*Recordame:	Joe Henderson
*Song for My Father:	Horace Silver
*Body and Soul:	Johnny Green
*Maiden Voyage:	Herbie Hancock
*I Love You:	Cole Porter
*Love For Sale:	Cole Porter
*Night and Day:	Cole Porter
*My Funny Valentine:	Rodgers and Hart
*It's You Or No One:	Chan and Styne
*Breezin':	George Benson

*Blue Monk: Thelonius Monk
*Bag's Groove: Milt Jackson
*Angel Eyes: Mat Dennis
*What Is This Thing Called Love: Cole Porter
*The Girl from Impanema: Antonio Carlos Jobim

*2007-2008 intended music to study

Chapter 10

Show Me the Money: Scholarships and Financial Aid

· ·

The financial aid process strikes fear in the hearts of many. Why? Because, from the outside looking into the labyrinth of forms, deadlines and requirements, the tasks seems Herculean. There are a plethora of resources for obtaining financial aid, need-based, merit-based and loans. The first stop truly should be the colleges themselves. College admissions officers are well aware that the price of a post-secondary education is prohibitive to many. They have trained financial aid officers to guide families through the mazes! Generally, there are several types of financial aid: merit-based and need-based grants and scholarships, loans and work-study programs.

MERIT-BASED AWARDS: SCHOLARSHIPS

Most students and parents do not realize the amazing amount of merit scholarships available. Colleges and universities across the

IN THIS CHAPTER

- Did you know that the vast majority of merit scholarships are awarded by individual colleges?

- Learn how to position yourself to receive thousands of dollars in merit awards, not loans, not grants and not work study

United States offer millions of dollars of merit-based scholarships every year. Many private schools will meet or come very close to meeting in-state public school tuition rates. Can you imagine? You can attend a private college or university for the same cost as you would pay to attend your state university! Even public colleges and universities have tiers of merit-based scholarship awards based on grades, SAT/ACT scores, and sometimes subjective criteria. You may be able to attend an out-of-state university for an in-state price.

Merit-based scholarships do not factor in any financial issues. They are based strictly on objective and subjective criteria including: grades, SAT/ACT scores, community service, leadership, etc. Lots of private schools are able and willing to offer this type of aid even to the more "average" students. Many of these schools offer merit-based awards in the initial interview or with the admissions acceptance letter.

In researching scholarships, start with college websites. The information will usually be under the heading of admissions or financial aid. Often the merit-based scholarships are laid out very clearly in tiers based on grade point averages and board scores. An example follows:

President's Scholars: $12,000 per year.

Minimum GPA: 3.75

Minimum SAT: 1250 (Critical Reading and Math)

Minimum ACT: 28

V.P. Scholars: $9,000 per year.

Minimum GPA: 3.50

Minimum SAT: 1150 (Critical Reading and Math)

Minimum ACT: 26

Trustee's Scholars:	$6,000 per year.
	Minimum GPA: 3.30
	Minimum SAT: 1100 (Critical Reading and Math)
	Minimum ACT: 24
Dean's Scholars:	$1,000 per year.
	Minimum GPA: 3.00
	Minimum SAT: 1000 (Critical Reading and Math)
	Minimum ACT: 22

Isn't it amazing how clearly this is laid out? As I mentioned earlier, some colleges even offer scholarship calculators online. These calculators allow students to plug in their board scores and grade point averages to develop a preliminary estimate of scholarship possibilities. If you are reading this early in your high school career, take a moment to search some college websites. The opportunities may encourage you to study just a bit harder in school and for your SAT/ACT exams. The efforts pay off in scholarship dollars earned.

In addition to the strictly academic scholarships based on grades and board scores, many schools offer leadership, service and community scholarships. These often require a separate application and a day or two at the college in a scholarship weekend or competition day.

How does one find and qualify for these scholarship opportunities? There is a very specific strategy to ferreting out merit-based awards.

1. Step back and think about the colleges' point of view. To whom will they offer the greatest scholarships? Colleges will essentially pay the students that they wish to attract. What does this mean to you?

Once again, you will need to look at your safety, attainable and reach schools. You have the best probability of receiving merit award money at your safety schools. Why? The colleges want to attract the students they see as elite. This does not mean that you have to be a 4.0+ student with perfect SAT/ACT scores at all. It means that you have to be significantly above the average admissions rate of your target school. For example, if you have a 3.5 GPA with an SAT score of 1150 (Critical Reading and Math), you will want to target schools with averages of 3.0 to 3.3 with SAT scores in the 1000 to 1050 range. In addition, your student resume must reflect your leadership skills, service activities and other college-attracting attributes. Think about how the colleges want to round out their student bodies.

2. Get going early! Apply as early as possible, preferably in August or September of your senior year. Many scholarship competitions begin in October or November.

3. Research. Spend some time on each individual college's website. Look at the scholarship, honors and any other special programs. If the website has an award calculator, use it to develop an estimate.

4. Look at your safety schools' honors programs. Many honors programs offer small classes within big universities, special perks such as early class registration and dormitory choice, plenty of academic rigor AND merit scholarships.

5. Interview early! Let the colleges know of your interest. Prepare for the interview by making sure all of the application requirements are submitted with your application. These include: application, essay, transcript, SAT/ACT scores, letters of recommendation, student resume, and application fee. In addition, bring hard copies of your transcript, SAT/ACT scores and student resume to your interview just in case.

6. Raise the issue of merit-based scholarships in your interview. If you have done your homework ahead of time and researched the college's scholarships and honors programs you will have a good leg up because you can ask the admissions officers about the specific scholarships that fit you. Don't be surprised though if the admissions officer raises the issue of merit scholarships before you have the chance. The colleges want to attract strong, involved students.

7. Dot your i's and cross your t's. What does this mean? It means that in order to maximize your scholarship potential, you will have to stand out above other students. So, how do I do this, you ask? If you have read Chapters 1 through Chapter 9, you already have the strategies. Make sure that you are offering the colleges an organized marketing package of your application, student and/or athletic/music/arts resumes and letters of recommendation. As we discussed earlier, your application should reflect strong organization and a clear focus on your passion and goals.

Let's take a look at one of our sample students, Grace Bennington. Grace's spreadsheet is the second one in Chapter 2, Developing Your Personal College List. Grace really liked the idea of a smaller college within four to five hours of her Washington, DC, home. She targeted two private schools (Lynchburg and Roanoke Colleges) and two public universities (Longwood and Christopher Newport). By interviewing and applying early, Grace put herself in a good position to discuss merit-based scholarship awards. In her initial interviews with the private colleges, Grace was offered merit money. In her acceptance letters, she received both awards of $12,000 to $15,000 and the opportunity to participate in additional scholarship contests at the schools. By October, Grace's award estimates decreased her total annual fees at the private schools from an average of $35,000 to approximately $15,000. She also competed for and earned a leadership scholarship from Christopher Newport University, a very desirable Virginia public university. So, Grace a good but not outstanding student, had offers of over $200,000 of four-year merit scholarships by October of her senior year.

Grace's case is not the exception. Colin McFimian, our University of Pittsburgh student had a similar experience (Colin's spreadsheet is the first one in Chapter 2). Colin targeted schools with strong pre-medicine programs and set his heart on the University of Pittsburgh, part of the Pennsylvania State Universities. Like Grace, Colin was not going to qualify for much need-based financial aid. He visited the University of Pittsburgh, developed a relationship and ended up with an $18,000 annual merit-based award along with a $3,000 annual need-based award. Colin now attends the University of Pittsburgh at the cost of $10,000 per year (the sticker price is $31,000). The $84,000 that Colin will save over four years will certainly help to cover the costs of medical school.

Another student, Portia, had grown up in an unfortunate home situation. After her parents' bitter divorce and several years of acrimonious aftermath, Portia made the difficult decision to leave home at 18 and make her way in the world. A very strong student with a 3.8 GPA and an approximately 1150 SAT (Critical Reading and Math), Portia figured that her only way to attend college would be to enroll in ROTC, take out student loans, apply for work study and find a part-time job. When Portia came to me for her help, she was convinced that she would owe the Army and the loan companies for the rest of her life. Looking at Portia's excellent resume with strong grades, SAT's, Girl Scouts, volunteer service and employment history, I knew that she would be a valuable asset to many colleges.

When I suggested to Portia that she consider some private colleges, her jaw dropped and she looked at me as if I were absolutely nuts. A little convincing, several calls and transmissions of Portia's resume and the colleges were competing for Portia's application. Our strategy to gain the most merit award scholarship money centered around looking at safety schools with ROTC programs on campus. Given Portia's GPA of 3.8, we knew that colleges with GPA's of 3.0 to 3.2 would be thrilled to have her. By forwarding Portia's student resume, SAT scores and transcripts, we allowed the admissions officers to gain some background and to discuss her potential and scholarship offers ahead of our visits.

On Portia's 18ᵗʰ birthday, we visited Mary Baldwin College (MBC), a small woman's college in the Blue Ridge Mountains of Virginia. We targeted MBC because of its strong reputation, history and its Virginia Women's Institute for Leadership, the only all female Corps of Cadets in the country. Portia arranged to spend the night at MBC to get a better feel for the college. The following morning, Portia took a tour of the campus and interviewed with an Admissions Dean. While Portia toured the school with a student representative, the Admissions Dean reviewed Portia's application along with her official transcript and SAT scores. When Portia returned from the tour, good news was awaiting her. MBC accepted her application and offered an initial merit scholarship of $16,000 (over 50% of the annual costs of $30,000). The ROTC recruiter who interviewed Portia assured her that she would qualify for the maximum annual Army ROTC scholarship of $19,000 plus a monthly stipend of $300 for spending money. In one morning, Portia had gone from significant financial worry to a completely financed college education with no student loans, work study or FAFSA form to complete.

While these stories may seem fantastic, they are not uncommon. There is an amazing amount of merit scholarship money available. You must plan and target appropriately. YOU CAN DO THIS!

DON'T BELIEVE THE URBAN LEGENDS

For some reason, many people do not believe that merit scholarships are available for students with middle class and greater incomes. If you mention that you are considering a merit scholarship, do not be surprised to hear from friends, family and even professionals that you will not qualify because your parents earn too much money. Let me give you two examples.

I'll start with Portia whom you have already met. Portia ran into several obstacles on her way to Mary Baldwin College. First, her mother, in an angry rage, tried to cancel Portia's application to Mary Baldwin. When the admissions officers did not allow that, she threatened to not sign the FAFSA form or any other parental forms that would support Portia's claim to have emancipated from her parents. That, of course, did not work either, as Portia had just turned 18 and Mary Baldwin did not require any more information from her parents.

After Portia returned from Mary Baldwin with a merit scholarship and her preliminary ROTC estimate, she and I went to visit her high school guidance counselor to share the great news and to set the wheels in motion to send the requisite secondary school reports to ROTC and Mary Baldwin College. When Portia told her guidance counselor that she had been offered a full scholarship between her ROTC and merit-based award, the guidance counselor pulled a sad face and hit Portia with the bad news. She told Portia that her parents earned "too much money" and that Portia could not qualify for the scholarships without filling out the Federal FAFSA forms. I interjected that Portia had earned a merit-based scholarship and that Mary Baldwin did not require any further income documentation. The guidance counselor went on to explain that ALL financial aid, whether need-based or merit-based required the completion of the Federal forms. I disagreed as courteously as I could, but the guidance counselor refused to accept my explanation. Portia looked like she had been kicked in the gut. As we left the office, I assured Portia that her guidance counselor had misinformed her and promised to call Mary Baldwin upon my return to the office. Needless to say, steam was pouring from my ears; this so-called qualified educator, Portia's lifeline in the guidance office, was egregiously incorrect in her understanding of merit-based awards. I called the Office of Financial Aid at Mary Baldwin to clarify the issue for Portia. The very lovely Director with whom I had arranged Portia's visit almost laughed at me. She said, "Julia, didn't you just write a book about this very issue? You know that Mary Baldwin does not need Portia to complete any other forms or a parent signature. We are offering a merit-based not a need-based award to Portia. You know the difference! Our offer stands."

What would Portia have done if I had not been with her to hear the outrageously incorrect information that her trained guidance counselor was giving her? Would she have given up on the scholarship completely? My goal in relating this story is not to excoriate the guidance counselor, but to warn you of the misconceptions about merit-based aid.

My next story is a little more mild. It just occurred yesterday on the Fourth of July. My family and I were at the community swim club and we ran into a family friend. As we have two children of the same age, our conversation soon turned to college and where our respective kids would be heading in just about a month. Our friend was bemoaning the cost of his older son's private school in New Hampshire. He said that the tuition is three times that of a Virginia public school. I asked him about merit scholarships and he said something along the lines that middle class people don't qualify for those; he said that they had not even bothered as he and his wife knew that their son would not qualify for any scholarships given their family income. We moved on to talking about the beautiful weather and the upcoming pool games.

Just for curiosity, this morning I visited the website of the college that his son is attending. I headed to the admissions and financial aid parts of the site, and lo and behold saw a whole array of merit-based scholarships. Now our friend owns several homes and travels abroad for pleasure frequently so he probably does not even need to look at any financial aid for his kids; still, his son may very well have qualified for a merit-based scholarship award.

NEED-BASED FINANCIAL AID

Need-based aid is completely on financial need. Need-based aid includes scholarships, grants, work-study jobs and loans. The process begins with the U.S. Department of Education's Free Application for Federal Student Aid (FAFSA) form. Many colleges will ask you to complete this form even if need-based aid seems out of context for your family. Even if your parents are absolutely sure that your family will not qualify for student aid, complete a FAFSA form anyway! Be sure to check with each college's individual financial aid offices for any supplemental financial aid forms. College financial aid officers are trained and knowledgeable in this field and are more than willing to help students. It is best to make an appointment with the financial aid officers ahead of time so that they can devote time and attention to your case.

Updated FAFSA forms are available January 1 of each year; they should be downloaded and completed after January 1st of your senior year. Although you should complete the FAFSA form as soon as possible, be aware that you will need to have your up-to-date annual Federal Tax Return completed in order to answer all the questions on the FAFSA form. Keep in mind that the early bird gets the worm. Since funds are limited at many schools, early submission of the FAFSA form maximizes your chances of receiving aid.

The FAFSA form is available on the web at www.fafsa.ed.gov. For paper copies, contact your high school guidance office, local library, or request by phone at 1-800-433-3243. A 2008 sample FAFSA form is included at the end of this chapter.

Karen Parker, Director for Virginia Women's Institute for Leadership/Athletic Recruitment at Mary Baldwin College in Staunton, Virginia, compiled the following list of do's and don'ts:

COMMON FAFSA ERRORS: DO'S AND DONT'S

1. DO sign the application. If you are filing as a dependent student, make sure your parents sign too. If you are filing electronically YOU and YOUR PARENTS must have a PIN number in order to sign the FAFSA form. Electronic PIN information: www.pin.ed.gov.

2. DO use the 1040 Federal tax return for reporting income and taxes paid, not the W-2. If this is not available, estimate your income by using paycheck stubs and asset information.

3. DO submit the FAFSA form even if you don't think you qualify for aid. Sometimes being rejected for federal aid is a prerequisite for receiving private awards.

4. DON'T leave a field blank. Use a zero if the question does not apply to you.

5. DON'T forget to report ALL required sources of untaxed income, such as social security or child support.

WHAT'S NEXT?

You should receive your Student Aid Report (SAR) in one to two weeks if filed electronically or four to six weeks if submitted by mail. Be sure to review this report CAREFULLY.

OTHER SCHOLARSHIP OPPORTUNITIES

In addition to the individual college's and universities' merit-based scholarships and financial aid need-based packages, there is a plethora of scholarships available nationally, regionally and locally.

RESEARCH OPPORTUNITIES

If you need financial aid, please begin your research process early. There are many websites and books available, as well as experts in the school system and in the college financial aid offices.

Professional Tutoring recommends the following resources

1. *College Financial Aid for Dummies*, by Davis and Kennedy.
2. Scholarshipsexperts.com
3. Fafsa.ed.gov
4. CollegeBoard.org
5. CollegeAnswer.com
6. Fastweb.com

Acknowledgments

Thank you for contributing your resumes, essays and stories:

Colin McGuire

Meredith Ross

Ally Mackin

Justin Griggs

Hailey Smith

Maggie Wright

Kelly Smith

Jessica Hogarth

Keith Askey

Vicki Malloy

Katie Morris

Brian Cahill

Patricia Patten, Christopher Newport University

Karen Parker, V.W.I.L., Mary Baldwin College

Thank you for editing, reviewing and encouraging:

Robin Hiddemen

Carl Plath

Mitch Aydlette

Melinda Villagran

Mark Feinsot

Richard Boone and Linda Brown

Renée Garrett

Kelly Coggshall

Jacqueline Grace and the LifeTime Media staff

Thank you for believing:

Jon Fuller

Finally, thank you to my family, committed and loving: David, Meredith, Emma, William, Terry and Kay

Julia Ross

NOTES

NOTES